Bev: *For my life partner, Paul, who gave me full access to his entire portfolio of wisdom, support, and love, throughout this project.*

Gaye: *To my family, Bruce, Colin, and Gwen, and to all of the teachers willing to share their commitment to children with Bev and me.*

> Contents

Acknowledgments

We wish to thank the following people for their invaluable contributions to our thinking and the writing of *Focused Portfolios™: A Complete Assessment for the Young Child:*

- Judy Harris Helm, Best Practices, Inc.
- Brenda Lee Smith, Child Care Connections
- Charmaine Espinosa and Judy Paiz, Children, Youth and Families Department, Office of Child Development, State of New Mexico
- Maria York and the families of Holy Trinity Christian Preschool, Streeter, Illinois
- Sharon Mann and the families of Westminster Infant Care Program, Peoria, Illinois
- Beth Hendricks and the families of Little Rainbows Preschool, Mackinaw, Illinois
- Lora Shull and the families of Sunburst Center of Child Development, Peoria Heights, Illinois
- Linda Desroches, Sara Maiorano, Cynthia Brissett-Loppie, Audrey Gee, and the families of the infants and toddlers of Centre de la Petite Enfance St. Mary's, Montréal, Québec
- Diana Tosi, Assistant Director, Gina Gasparrini, Director, Centre de la Petite Enfance St. Mary's, Montréal, Québec
- Louise Fitzpatrick, Diana Battiste, Angi Casler, Connie Jones-McLean, Michael Paulone, Camille Cass, Cynthia Reynolds, Sharon Mealka, Patricia Collins, Kelli Jo Hancock, Curtis Sigafoose, Lucy Kramer, and the families of the Indiana School for the Deaf, Indianapolis, Indiana
- Sandra Warner, Elizabeth Kinser, Veronica Cisowski, Melissa D'Agostino, Nelida Frontera, Pam Giermann, Gerlinde Janowski, Anji Persico, Heidi Wagreich, Jan Batchelor, Shirley Justin-Wolff, Debi Kowske, Kathy Bentham, Gloria Contreras, Lidia Contreras, Tanya Contreras, Cosme Encinas, Araceli Hernandez, Sandy Horvath, Laura Jacques, Gloria Oyarce, Armando Padilla, Crystal Setzke, Debbie Simmons, Eileen Tarter, Laurie Woodbury, and the families of West Chicago Community School District #33, West Chicago, Illinois

- Eduardo Fuentes of West Chicago for Spanish translations
- Martha Inch, Orcas Island, Washington
- Linda Housewright and the families of Dallas Community School District #336, Dallas City, Illinois
- Karen Sullivan, Donna Nylander, and the teachers and families of Prairie Children Preschool, Naperville, Illinois
- Sue Reed, former Director of The Children's Center at the University of New England, Portland, Maine
- Christine Durocher, Director, Centre de la Petite Enfance Tchou-Tchou for French translations and samples
- Susan Busker, Jayne Erikson, Evelyn Freeman, and the families of Rockford Public Schools Early Childhood Program, Rockford, Illinois
- Debbie Highsmith, Bruce Nowlin, teachers and families at USA Group Kids, Bright Horizons Family Solutions, Indianapolis, Indiana
- Allyson Dean, Kevin Dean, Caitlin Salpietra, Stephanie Lumsden, Alice Cousins, Melissa Malloy, and Lucy and Tom Manderson of University of Southern Maine Child Care Center
- Sonja Howard, Stephen White, and Melissa Pettingill, The Children's Center at Westbrook College, Portland, Maine
- Teachers at Las Cumbres Specialized Learning Services, Espanola, New Mexico
- Marie Salas, Deanna Walker, and teachers at Springer Early Care and Education Center, Springer, New Mexico
- Karen Rodberg, Mary Smiley, and teachers of Central Consolidated Schools, Shiprock, New Mexico
- Teachers at Shima Yazhi Home Visiting Program at the Gathering Place, Thoreau, New Mexico
- Peggy Koukos, Betsy Lane, Susan Muzzy, Matt Voyer, and Cindy Greelie of First Lutheran Preschool, Portland, Maine
- Marjorie Wilson, Luz Marchand, Carol Goss, Sandy Palmer, Pat Flanagan, all of Child Care of Southwest Florida
- Luisa Iglio, Director, Janice Picard, Aline Karagioules, and Jennifer Bellware of Centre de la Petite Enfance Dorval, Dorval, Québec
- Stephanie and Michael Drinan
- Mary and Jon Gorham
- Mary and Todd Grove
- Michelle Fournier and Lauritz Dyhrberg

> Introduction

Teachers and administrators of early childhood programs in the United States and Canada have told us that comprehensive assessment tools are essential to enhancing the quality of their services. Accreditation requirements, as well as new emphasis on accountability, have created a need for improved methods to document children's growth and development. These professionals want an authentic assessment approach—something that is not artificially imposed on children.

We have heard time and again that teachers are attracted to the idea of portfolios but worry about what "stuff" they should collect and how much time it will take to do so. Most point out that meeting children's needs is their goal and requires their full-time attention. These teachers worry that documenting their regular observations will be an obstacle to being fully involved with the children.

Those who are already trying to compile portfolios are experiencing what they characterize as the stresses of endless filing and storing of photos, work samples, and anecdotes; financing cameras, film, and film processing; and interrupting children so teachers can document what they are doing.

We were convinced that we could develop a simple and efficient process of portfolio collection based on authentically documenting the daily experiences of children in their away-from-home settings.

We understood that teachers were already observing children but not always writing down what they saw and heard. We believed they really wanted a straightforward tool to help them focus and record their observations and connect them to accepted developmental expectations for children. Our response was to design the Focused Portfolios™ process.

> This Book

This book, then, is intended for early childhood educators of infants, toddlers, and preschoolers in child care centers, Head Start programs, and nursery schools and family child care. Our goal is to make it simple, straightforward, and teacher-friendly. We identify steps in the process of portfolio planning, collection, selection, and conferencing with families. We share helpful hints and strategies to make the process informative and efficient, yet easy to implement. We want to help teachers get organized so they can systematically record observations, collect samples of children's work, and take photographs. The portfolio tells a complete story about each child's experience in an early childhood setting.

We conceived the Focused Portfolios™ process in the belief that by designing a structured and planned approach to documenting children's growth and development, we could accomplish the following:

- provide an efficient, teacher- and family-friendly, easy-to-manage portfolio process
- influence teachers to focus on developmental milestones when observing, documenting, and planning curriculum
- provide an informative developmental keepsake for families
- assist teachers in planning individualized curriculum
- encourage teachers to use a mechanism that could account for and explain what they plan and do with and for young children

Throughout the book we refer to "groups," "programs," and "classrooms." We use the term "teachers" to mean any adult who cares for and educates young children. We know that there are many other titles, such as caregivers, educators, child care workers, lead teachers, head teachers, assistant teachers, and family child care providers. We use the term "teacher" throughout because all adults who work with young children are teachers in some sense.

> What Is the Focused Portfolios™ Process?

The Focused Portfolios™ process asks teachers to authentically assess children by carefully observing them in everyday interactions in the classroom. This observation happens in the natural context of teaching and providing care. When diapering an infant, snuggling with a toddler, assisting a young preschooler with a puzzle, or reading a story with a four-year-old, teachers are learning about each child's development. This book shows teachers how to put together a simple but comprehensive portfolio to capture that learning, to document observations, and to relate the child's development to recognized milestones.

All the necessary forms for portfolio collection are included in this book. These are the basis for reporting to families and reflecting on curriculum. These forms, used in combination with photographs, work samples, and anecdotes, make up a completed Focused Portfolios™ set.

The Focused Portfolios™ assessment is unique in the following ways:

- We have designed easy-to-use formats for putting together a portfolio, complete with forms and fill-in-the-blank sheets that can be photocopied and tailored to individual children.
- We have included forms to correlate the portfolio to identified goals for young children with special needs (Individual Family Service Plans—IFSPs, and Individual Education Plans—IEPs).
- This book includes two sample Focused Portfolios™ collections as well as numerous other examples. By looking through these, teachers don't have to guess or figure out what we are inviting them to do. We explain it and we show how to accomplish it.
- We offer tips to help organize and store photos and children's work. We make suggestions to keep the work manageable, meaningful, and enjoyable.
- This book includes simple and straightforward instructions for starting to use the Focused Portfolios™ approach. Teachers have told us that the single biggest obstacle to using an assessment tool is feeling overwhelmed by "too much, too soon." For that reason, we have carefully presented the steps for using the Focused Portfolios™ process in a way that allows teachers to become very comfortable with the basic format.

It is our firm belief that with early success comes the willingness to continue. Once the basics are "comfortably under a teacher's belt," the scope can be broadened, and more depth can be introduced. For this reason, some of the chapters have basic information for getting started as well as "Ideas for Experienced Users." With new suggestions and examples supplied, teachers can further augment their skills and continue to enhance classroom planning and the quality of interactions with children and their respective families.

> Why Use the Focused Portfolios™ Approach?

From our own classroom experiences, and from the reports of the many teachers with whom we have worked, we believe observing and documenting children's development in a structured way can make teachers' and administrators' jobs easier.

Classrooms run more smoothly when children's needs are met. This portfolio process will become a guide to help write daily plans and individualize programs to meet each child's needs.

Observing helps teachers know children better. By closely watching everything children do in the classroom, teachers can see development in action clearly. This deeper understanding helps meet children's needs and makes the task of working in early childhood programs more satisfying and interesting.

Providing photographs along with descriptions of everyday classroom activities helps families gain understanding of their children's experiences while away from home. These concrete illustrations generate focused discussions between family members and teachers and facilitate shared goal setting for the child. Teachers and administrators report deeper connections to families as a result of this partnering and more support for the program.

Sharing the documentation in the portfolios also says a lot about an early childhood professional. By documenting the child's experience in the program, the teacher demonstrates her willingness to share what happens in her classroom. That raises accountability and provides a learning opportunity for all who contribute to and see the end of the Focused Portfolios™ process. It says that the teacher is open to having others witness her particular interpretation of developmentally appropriate early childhood education. Documentation invites authentic conversations about what each child has experienced and achieved in the classroom and what next steps make sense for each child.

Directors interviewing prospective teachers can share the Developmental Milestones in the Focused Portfolios™ process, and use them as a vehicle for determining whether there is a fit between what the program values and what the teacher believes is important for young children.

When the Focused Portfolios™ approach to assessment is clearly defined and described as part of the program's expectations for staff, the teachers feel more confident about their jobs. This may contribute to greater teacher retention.

When there is staff turnover, having a concrete format of documentation in place can minimize the disruptive effects. New teachers will have information about the children in their classroom, as well as about the curriculum.

The documentation in each portfolio will help new staff identify a place to start and a direction to go in their work with the children. They'll have a jump start on what each child can do, is interested in, and is working toward achieving.

When new teachers are introduced to children through the Focused Portfolios™ process, transition and orientation time is reduced and the new teacher is able to more quickly establish an individual relationship with each child.

> About the Authors

Each of us has worn many hats in our early childhood education careers: preschool teachers in a variety of settings (including Head Start, college laboratory schools, cooperative nursery schools, child care centers, and special education classrooms), college instructors, and staff development consultants to early childhood programs around North America. As classroom teachers, we were both attracted to authentic performance assessment as the most child-friendly way to learn about and document children's development. We practiced observation and note taking and tried out various portfolio formats.

As college instructors and consultants, we have helped thousands of teachers implement these important assessment practices. We have come to believe that portfolios based on observations and sound developmental principles can provide a window into the learning that happens in care and education settings. We have learned much from our own classroom experiences, as well as from the teachers with whom we have consulted. We feel certain that if more people are helped to see what good early childhood programs accomplish, the field and all its teachers will be the beneficiaries.

> Field Testing

In 1998–99, we were fortunate enough to have fifteen teachers in Peoria, Illinois, and four in Montréal, Québec, field-test the Focused Portfolios™ process. From their work, two Focused Portfolios™ collections, plus numerous samples, are included in this book. These teachers' experiences and suggestions helped us to keep coming back to what was realistic in most early childhood settings. The field testing has also enabled us to give you a firsthand account of how it has worked in many actual classroom settings.

Since January 2000, many more programs in the United States and Canada have been using this portfolio format. The State of New Mexico Office of Child Development has officially adopted the Focused Portfolios™ assessment tool for all state-funded child care programs. Many child care centers, university lab schools, prekindergarten at-risk programs, bilingual early childhood, and special education classrooms are implementing the process. We are in contact with teachers in most of these programs and continually learn from their experiences. We are grateful for their feedback, shared samples, and stories of both successes and challenges. We have included many of their reflections and insights throughout this book.

chapter 1

Favorites Collection Form
Child's Name Brandon
Observer Beth
Date October 1998
cup into
ger bowl.
grate the
, and had

> The Focused Portfolios™ Process

A portfolio is a way to document or keep track of a child's ongoing development. By saving samples of a child's work and writing anecdotes about his interactions, a teacher puts together evidence of a child's learning and accomplishments.

Portfolios are well accepted as a type of "authentic assessment." Authentic assessment means evaluating children's growth through their daily activities, instead of using something that is not part of their regular routine, such as standardized tests. Teachers choose authentic assessment because they believe that everyday experiences most accurately show what children have learned and the progress they have made.

We have found that many teachers are interested in using portfolios but find the process overwhelming and time-consuming. We designed the Focused Portfolios™ process with that concern in mind. It offers teachers of children birth to age five a planned and organized format that is easy to fit into a busy day.

From working with many early childhood teachers, we know that your job is already demanding. You're on your feet long hours. You're attentive to the children on a nonstop basis. Your daily task list is lengthy and time-consuming. The Focused Portfolios™ process will not add overwhelming storage and filing problems. This assessment tool will be woven into your daily routines with children and will help you evaluate, celebrate, and enjoy children's development.

> What Is the Focused Portfolios™ Process?

The Focused Portfolios™ process is a framework for creating early childhood portfolios. It offers structure and guidance for teachers who are ready to plan and implement authentic assessment within developmentally appropriate programs.

A portfolio that is put together using this process is a planned collection of "documentation" about a child. Documentation is evidence of a child's experience and includes photos of the child in action, or work samples that the child produced. To go along with each photo and work sample, the teacher writes an "anecdote"—a note describing what was happening with the child at the time the photo was taken or the work sample was made.

The Focused Portfolios™ process is not a blueprint for compiling a scrapbook or a photo album, nor does it limit the scope of a portfolio to a random collection of artwork and writing samples.

Teachers collect specific pieces of documentation over several months. Two or three times a year they pull together what they have collected and prepare a Reflection and Planning Form, which evaluates the child's accomplishments and progress. This report and the portfolio are then shared with each child's family. Teachers and family members conference to set goals and make plans to support each child's growth both at home and in the early childhood program setting.

Using the Focused Portfolios™ process, teachers collect documentation in four categories: favorites, friends, family, and developmental milestones. These four categories show teachers and family members what children's interests and strengths are. Documenting accepted developmental milestones helps look at children's performance in relation to age-appropriate expectations. The framework is the same for infants, toddlers, and preschoolers.

There are many excellent charts and checklists of developmental milestones and widely held expectations for young children. The Developmental Milestones Charts in this book are adapted from *Developmentally*

Appropriate Practice in Early Childhood Programs (Revised Edition) by Sue Bredekamp and Carol Copple, published by the National Association for the Education of Young Children (NAEYC). For preschoolers, supplemental milestones are drawn from another source: *The Primary Program: Growing and Learning in the Heartland* (State Departments of Education for Iowa and Nebraska). This is the same source that the authors of the NAEYC book relied on for preschool information.

There were several reasons for selecting these sources:

- These references set the standard of developmentally appropriate practice for the field of early childhood education.
- The books are readily available and widely used by early childhood programs and are therefore familiar to many practitioners.
- The milestones in these sources apply to the age range birth to age five (infants, toddlers, and preschoolers).
- The number of milestones provided for each age range is not overwhelming.
- The information can apply to both typically developing children as well as those with identified special needs.

If you already are using a different developmental checklist or resource, you can still apply this portfolio process in your program. Or if, after reviewing the milestone information in this book, you wish to select another source of developmental information, the Focused Portfolios™ system can be adapted to address any developmental milestones a program chooses. *(See appendix C for examples.)*

> How to Collect Documentation

Documentation is made up of four parts:

1. Observing a child or a group of children
2. Writing down what you see and hear: the anecdote
3. Taking a photo or selecting a child's work sample
4. Putting the anecdote and photo or work sample together on the collection forms

Specially designed collection forms for documenting children's favorites, friends, family, and developmental milestones are included in this book. Collection forms for documenting progress toward goals for young children with identified special needs (Individual Family Service Plan [IFSP] and Individual Education Plan [IEP] goals) are also included. Chapters 2 and 4 give you specific information about how to collect work samples and photographs and write anecdotes on these forms. These chapters also have many examples of completed documentation to guide you. In addition, two sample collections for two different children are included in chapters 3 and 6.

For infants and toddlers, photographs accompanied by teacher-written anecdotes or stand-alone anecdotes will be most common. Infants and toddlers just don't produce much on paper because they're too busy exploring the world around them. It would be inappropriate to expect otherwise or to interfere with what they do naturally. Photos and anecdotes are the best way to capture their learning as it unfolds.

Because preschoolers are able to represent more of their learning and knowledge, paintings, drawings, and writing samples will also be included.

For both age groups, teachers write detailed descriptions of children's activities and direct quotes of their oral language. These "stand-alone anecdotes" are also effective and powerful forms of documentation.

Even though the format for this type of portfolio is the same for all children, the pieces of documentation collected will be different for each child. No two portfolios will look exactly the same. Each will tell a distinctive story and include the unique ways in which children show their accomplishments, interests, and personalities.

The chapters that follow will help you become competent at observing and writing anecdotes, taking good photos, effectively sharing with families, and using the information collected to plan accordingly. We've also included suggestions for addressing progress and making changes in second and subsequent collections.

We have worked with many teachers who are implementing this assessment tool. Throughout the book, we include their stories and suggestions to help you learn the Focused Portfolios™ process. We also recognize that, like children, adults have their own pace of absorbing new ideas and information. Therefore, we have separated out some suggestions as "Ideas for Experienced Users" and invite you to make use of these when you feel ready to go beyond the basics.

> Getting Started

Planning is the key to ensuring that observing and recording become regular parts of your routine. If you are well prepared, then collecting documentation will be smooth and hassle-free. Here are basic steps for gathering the necessary materials and getting started with the Focused Portfolios™ process.

Steps	Recommendations
1. Choose a method for storing photos, anecdotes, and work samples.	Set up a file folder or three-ring binder for each child (for photos and anecdotes), labeled with the child's name. Because preschoolers and older toddlers produce work samples (such as large paintings), you may also want a hanging file, cardboard box, plastic crate, or pizza box for each child in which to store those samples.
2. Determine a classroom location where these files and work samples will be stored.	The children's portfolio file folders should be kept in an out-of-the-way place so that they will be safe and ready to share with family members (e.g., a file or desk drawer, a magazine library case, or a plastic milk crate).
3. Decide on the number of times during the year you will meet with families to share the portfolios.	If the children attend your program for a nine- or ten-month session, collecting two sets of items and meeting twice with families is sufficient to document and discuss progress. If the program runs year-round, then collecting three sets of items provides a more informative, accurate, and continuous picture of each child's progress over the course of a year. *(See Sample Calendars in chapter 8.)*
4. Organize the following tools and materials before beginning the portfolio process: cameras, film, film-processing arrangements, photocopies of collection forms, staplers, audiotapes and recorders, and videotapes and recorders.	1. Have a camera in each classroom. Due to the cost of film, we recommend a 35-millimeter camera. Instant cameras are easy and convenient to use, but the cost of film is high. Digital cameras are beginning to drop in price. Some programs are finding them very reasonable as a long-term investment. *(For ideas on how to fund film and film processing, see suggestions at the end of this chapter.)* 2. Acquire film and have several rolls on hand. A roll of 36 photos per child for the year will provide more than enough shots to document developmental milestones and other events that occur, and will allow for occasional goofs or poor quality. *Continued on next page*

Steps	Recommendations
Continued from previous page	3. Arrange for film processing. Teachers tell us that high-volume photo processors (e.g., Wal-Mart or Sam's Club) offer the lowest prices for photo finishing. We suggest that if family members contribute by buying film, you ask them to arrange for prepaid processing or provide you with film-processing coupons. Before you begin the portfolio process, your program can set up a volume account with the store you plan to use. 4. For each child, make at least one photocopy of each of the collection forms for Friends, Favorites, and Family and file these three forms in each child's folder. *(See chapter 2.)* 5. For each child, make at least seven photocopies of the Developmental Milestones Collection Form *(see chapter 2)* and file these seven forms in each child's file folder. Suggestion: Photocopying Developmental Milestones Collection Forms on seven different colors of paper (a different color for each area of development) makes it easier to put your hands on the correct form and adds to the attractiveness of the portfolio. This is optional. 6. Photocopy several copies of the Focused Portfolios™ Photo Form to have ready when you need them *(see more in chapter 2)*. These can be stored in a file labeled "Photo Forms" in your file cabinet or desk drawer. 7. Acquire a stapler for teacher use. This will be used to staple photos and work samples to the collection forms. 8. Acquire audiotapes, videotapes, and recorders (optional).
5. Prepare to use developmental milestones.	1. Become familiar with the Developmental Milestones Charts. *(See chapter 2.)* 2. Think about recommended ways to document developmental milestones. *(See the "Recommended Types of Documentation" tables in chapter 2.)*

Steps	Recommendations
6. Plan for observation.	Make the following decisions: • When will you fit it in? • How will you write it down? Throughout the book, many suggestions are given to help you with this planning process.
7. Try things out. All new learning requires a time of exploration and trial and error. It will take you a while to develop your own efficiency and expertise at effective portfolio documentation.	Give yourself permission to make some mistakes, to explore the process, to make adaptations for your program setting, and to learn what makes the most effective documentation.

How to Fund Cameras, Film, and Film Processing

Involve the families. Many programs have found this to be a wonderful opportunity to stimulate parent involvement because the rewards are so satisfying. Families love to see the portfolios. And, for that reason, they typically welcome being included in purchasing and processing rolls of film.

Sharon Mann, teacher/director at Westminster Infant Care Center in Peoria, Illinois, felt she could ask her teenage moms and dads to contribute $10 a year toward film and developing. These young parents recognized the worth of this investment and the value of the information they were receiving from the portfolios.

Many teachers and child care providers ask family members to contribute one roll of film and one film-processing coupon upon enrollment and then subsequently per year. That adds up to twenty-four to thirty-six photos of each child for the year. Families can give film and film-processing coupons to teachers as holiday gifts. The use of digital photography and instant cameras are options to be considered. Because of the cost of digital cameras, printers, photo paper, and film for instant cameras, each program will have to make decisions based on available financial resources.

chapter 2

Favorites Collection Form
Child's Name Brandon
Observer Beth
Date October 1998

> Documenting Favorites, Friends, Family, and Developmental Milestones

Once you're organized, you are ready to begin the portfolio process. This chapter introduces the basics of collecting documentation for favorites, friends, family, and developmental milestones. Chapter 3 contains a sample of a basic collection for a child so that you can see all of the information in this chapter demonstrated in an actual portfolio. More details about the documentation process are discussed in chapter 4.

Collecting items can happen spontaneously in the classroom or in your conversations with family members. Have your camera and collection forms ready and try to capture the moments as they occur. It can also be carefully planned ahead of time. You decide how the collection process best fits into your regular routine.

> Favorites

Capturing a record of a child's favorites is an important way to learn more about the child's unique interests, talents, and passions. What a child chooses to do again and again provides insight as to her emerging skills and competencies. Documenting those choices contributes to more individualized curriculum because the teacher can build upon each child's consistent choices and interest in planned activities.

Families are eager for information about how their children spend time away from home. One of the questions that family members often ask their child's teacher is "What is her favorite activity?" Sometimes a child's favorite activities and interests at school may be different from those the family sees at home. Other times, they may be the same. Collecting examples of children's favorites for the portfolio gives teachers and family members an opportunity to focus together on children's preferences and strengths.

Teachers can use the information gained by observing children's favorite activities to generate ideas about how to best support or challenge a child. Some teachers raise concerns about children who make the same choice of activity day after day. They think it may be best to encourage, or even demand, that the child move on and try new things, rather than returning again and again to the same activity. Before a teacher decides to take action, we recommend that she record the child's pattern of choices on the Favorites Collection Form. Then she can reflect on what she has seen and determine if it is in the child's best interest to intervene or not.

A toddler who repeatedly wants the same set of sorting blocks may be choosing an activity that is on the cusp of her development: repetition helps her develop the necessary skills to accomplish this task. After careful observation, the teacher may decide that it is best to support the child's choice so that the child can practice sorting. The teacher may also determine that some adult help would benefit the child's mastery of those skills. As she sees the child achieving success, the teacher provides the next level of challenge by offering more complex sorting activities. Observing and documenting each child's favorites can guide these curricular decisions.

Children's choices also indicate their interests. Many teachers report that over the years, they have had young "dinosaur or superhero experts": children who know all of the names and characteristics of dinosaurs or various superheroes, and continually talk about and reenact these themes in all of their play. Other teachers recognize that numerous aspects of daily life often capture the interest of young children: insects and spiders, puddles after a rainstorm or piles of snow after a blizzard, construction machinery, or types of transportation. By recording interest in such topics on the Favorites Collection Form, teachers have documentation to help them make planning decisions related to choice of curricular themes, materials, or furniture arrangement that can build on children's interests. Children are typically motivated to participate and become deeply engaged in activities that are tied directly to their interests.

Children's unique talents also can be evidenced in their consistent choices of favorites. Some children demonstrate their artistic capabilities or their increasing coordination and athleticism through favorite activities in which they participate again and again.

Some teachers have devised ways to keep track of children's choices so that favorite activities can be accurately identified. Melissa D'Agostino of the West Chicago Early Childhood Program follows the High/Scope Curriculum and uses the structure of "Plan, Do, and Review" with the children. During Review Time, each child points to or talks about the activities that he visited that morning or afternoon. Melissa records this information on a special Daily Report Form that she then photocopies to send home with the child. Additional notes about the day's events are included. After several weeks have passed, Melissa reviews these forms to identify each child's most frequently chosen activities.

> Friends

Young children's growing social competence is an important part of their overall development, and so it must be documented. Because so much of a child's social interaction occurs away from home, documentation in the category of Friends becomes an essential source of information for families.

Friends are another form of favorites. Children have special friends whom they seek out during the day. They may carefully watch or play alongside those friends. As children grow and mature, and as their verbal ability increases, their social interactions become more skillful. As they work and play with friends, they are more willing and able to share, take turns, and cooperate in solving the everyday problems that arise among peers.

When teachers pay attention to a child's interactions with other children, they gain useful information. They can determine strategies for guiding behavior and assisting children in establishing a sense of belonging. For example, infants and toddlers may watch particular children more closely than others. Or they may have specific adults to whom they are drawn. This is usually evidence of their desire to be social or the way in which they learn to imitate others. Teachers can support this early social development by placing infants in close proximity to each other. *(See the Mariah example later in this chapter.)* Facilitating play among toddlers who naturally gravitate toward each other helps foster socialization. For the Friends part of the portfolio, teachers record the people in the classroom in whom the child shows interest.

Preschoolers new to a program often benefit from having a "special friend" to help them get acquainted with the classroom and routines. Children who feel secure in a setting will take more risks and try new things. Children who are comfortable with others may stay engaged in activities longer, practice negotiation and compromise, and develop greater self-confidence. These behaviors and characteristics foster self-esteem and the ability to develop friendships. We urge teachers to use the Friends Collection Form to record their observations of children engaged in these ways.

Many teachers find that they must wait to fill out both the Favorites and Friends Collection Forms until they have gotten to know the children better. Because both of these items capture patterns of behavior rather than a single incident, Linda Desroches and Audrey Gee at Centre de la Petite Enfance St. Mary's in Montréal chose to postpone writing about them until their infants had settled in and were comfortable with others in the group. Using the Friends Collection Form to document social interaction allows both teachers and family members to see how social competence emerges and grows.

> Family

Because you are in a partnership with each child's family, you can either invite them to participate in compiling the portfolio or initiate a form of family recognition in the collection. A family's contribution may include any of the following:

- photographs accompanied by a description of a family outing or celebration
- the story of the birth of a sibling or the arrival of a family pet
- the explanation of how the child's name was chosen
- a grandparent's account of how the family members came to this country (in writing or on audiotape or videotape)

Some teachers send home a letter asking families to participate in the Focused Portfolios™ process. In it, they provide a list of suggestions like those above. In this way, family members can choose to create a portfolio item similar to one suggested, or they can generate other, more personalized ideas for their portfolio contribution.

In response to such a request, one of the parents in Angi Casler's preschool classroom at the Indiana School for the Deaf in Indianapolis sent back a letter that she had written to her child. The letter described how much the child meant to the mother, and some of the significant times in their relationship. Angi attached this letter to the Family Collection Form and found that from it, she learned a great deal about the child's early development and strong family support.

Here are some additional suggestions for involving families in portfolio collection:

- Teachers send home a resealable plastic bag with children who are leaving on a trip. A note is included asking them to bring back some object associated with an experience the family had while away from home (such as sand from the beach, a paper umbrella from an exotic drink that the child was served, or a photo of the family building a sand castle or swimming in the ocean).
- The children take turns bringing a backpack home for the weekend. It contains the class Teddy bear, a notebook, a disposable camera, and any objects from the classroom that the child thinks the Teddy will need while away for the weekend. The family keeps a journal (in the notebook provided) about the Teddy's adventures with the family and takes accompanying photos to document where the Teddy went. When the child returns after the weekend, the documentation helps him talk about what he and his family did.
- In another class, Figaro, a very long stuffed snake, and a library book chosen by the child, go home overnight. A family member and the child wrap Figaro around themselves while they read the book. If possible, a photo is taken while this occurs.
- Each family takes home a disposable camera and is invited to take a limited number of photos of "family life."
- Families are asked to write about how they celebrate various holidays and include any artifacts or holiday symbols that are associated with the celebration.
- Family members in Veronica Cisowski's bilingual classroom in West Chicago are asked to fill out a survey about their family life.

Not all families will have the time or wherewithal to make a contribution to the portfolio. When this occurs, you, as the teacher, may take the initiative to complete a Family Collection Form by

- photographing a family member's visit to the classroom to have lunch
- inviting family members to the classroom to share a special craft or skill (cooking, weaving, playing an instrument, etc.) with the children. The family member is photographed while engaged with the child or is asked to write about her experience or dictate it to the teacher.
- writing a description about the news the child has shared about a special family trip or visitor
- inviting families to school for a pancake breakfast or a pumpkin-carving night and taking photos of everyone together
- taking a photo of pick-up or drop-off routines
- noting what families include in children's lunches or snacks

In Diana Battiste's toddler class at the Indiana School for the Deaf, one mother brought the youngest of her seven children to school every day. Diana took a picture of their arrival and described this mother's dedication on the Family Collection Form. Diana wanted to affirm this mother's priorities and efforts on behalf of her child.

Whichever way a family chooses to become involved, or whatever way you can recognize their important contribution to their child's well-being, will enhance the home/school relationship and raise the child's self-esteem. By including these contributions in the portfolio, you are recognizing and celebrating the importance of family in the child's life.

In Sharon Mann's teen-parenting program in Peoria, Illinois, the photos she took of the teen moms and dads with their children took on great significance for the parents. Sharon reported that many of these photos decorated the middle-school and high-school lockers of these moms and dads. Through her portfolio process she had contributed documentation that became a significant source of pride for these young parents. She provided opportunities to these teenagers to learn more about typical expectations for their children, and modeled for them the ways she and her staff supported children's development. Including the parents in the Family piece of the portfolio helped them to begin to take some credit and pride in parenthood.

Some of the programs already using the Focused Portfolios™ process have found that the Family piece is a way to incorporate information about a child's culture. Home visitors for the Shima Yazhi program in New Mexico include stories in the portfolios about families' involvement in special celebrations and powwows. These stories tell about children sitting side-by-side with family members weaving at a loom or cooking Kneeldown Bread when corn is harvested.

Mary Smiley, a teacher for Central Consolidated Schools in Shiprock, New Mexico, asked families to respond to a questionnaire about their family activities and interests, as well as fill out a family tree. In Navajo culture, extended family and clan are an important way to celebrate connectedness. Mary took this into account when she planned how she wanted to recognize the families in the portfolio.

Several teachers have found that the children actively engage with the Friends and Family portfolio pieces when given access to them. Melissa D'Agostino has created a "Friends and Families Bulletin Board" *(see photo)* and finds that children visit it often. They point out photos depicting their own friends and family members, and talk with each other about them. Some teachers have chosen to assemble a family book or photo album for each child. These books then become part of the classroom library and are often the most popular items to read.

> How to Collect Items That Document Favorites, Friends, and Family

For collection of photos, work samples, and anecdotes for the portfolio, we have provided you with special collection forms for Favorites, Friends, and Family, which appear on the following pages. *(Forms ready for photocopying appear in appendix A; forms in Spanish can be found in appendix B.)*

Favorites Collection Form

Child's Name ______________________________ Date ________________________

Observer ________________________

After observing the child on multiple occasions, describe a favorite activity that the child does often. Add details that you've noticed about the child's interests and choices. Add a photo if you can.

Description:

Friends Collection Form

Child's Name ______________________________ Date ______________________

Observer _______________________

Based on your observations, who are this child's friends? What do they do together? How does this child express his or her feelings towards them? Add a photo to illustrate this friendship.

Description:

Family Collection Form

Child's Name ______________________________ Date ________________________

Observer ________________________

Families often have stories to share about their child's accomplishments at home. They also have special moments with their child in your classroom. Use this form to document a story that the child's family has shared with you, or take a photo of a special moment between the child and the people who are important in his or her life.

Description:

Before beginning the Focused Portfolios™ process, make a photocopy of each of these collection forms for each child. Fill in the child's name and place the three forms in the child's portfolio file. Your files should be located in a handy place in the classroom. In that way, they are close at hand and you are ready to go.

As you get to know your children better and have observed them enough to know what their favorites and who their friends are, you may take a photograph and write an anecdote right on the Favorites and Friends Collection Forms. It is usually best to fill out the collection form as soon as you have observed often enough to identify patterns of favorites and friends. You can add the photo once it is developed. Some teachers find it more convenient to write their observation on a sticky note instead of on the collection form. They have learned to write as legibly as possible so that this note can then be attached to the collection form at a later time. No rewriting is necessary. And sticky notepads are easier to carry in a pocket or have placed around the classroom for easy access.

At Little Rainbows Preschool in Mackinaw, Illinois, Beth Hendricks's portfolios contain several photos of the children in action with sticky-note anecdotes attached. When it gets closer to the time for family conferencing, Beth goes through these notes and photos and begins the process of filling out the appropriate forms.

For preschoolers, a work sample may be collected instead of a photo. This will most likely apply to observation of children's favorites, rather than their friends and family. You still fill out the collection form (or place a sticky note on it) and staple it directly to the child's work. In this case, there's no waiting for photography development.

Sometimes your description or story about favorites, friends, or family is lengthy. On the following page is a Focused Portfolios™ Photo form. This is to be used when you need an additional page to attach the photograph. If this is the case, staple the photo form to the Favorites, Friends, or Family form, and your documentation is ready to file.

Focused Portfolios™ Photo

Attach
photograph
here

> Examples of Favorites, Friends, and Family

Here are some examples of completed Favorites, Friends, and Family Collection Forms. Read the anecdotes carefully. Look at the different ways teachers have documented these important parts of children's development. Think about your children's interests, likes and dislikes, attempts at socialization and building friendships, and family relationships and cultural traditions. How will you be documenting these areas in your program?

Favorites Collection Form

Child's Name Alexandra Date March 30, 1999

Observer Sara

After observing the child on multiple occasions, describe a favorite activity that the child does often. Add details that you've noticed about the child's interests and choices. Add a photo if you can.

Description:

Alex's favorite activity is pretend play. Although she stays in various areas of the room, none captures her attention as fully as dramatic play. She often stays at this area for more than half an hour. She'll set the small table, invite friends, or even play on her own. As soon as we switch the drama centers (e.g., medical office, home living center, etc.) she'll be one of the first to explore and create scenarios!

Here, Alex says, "Look, we're lions". Together she and Katherine make a roaring sound.

(Alexandra is on the right)

Favorites Collection Form

Child's Name Brandon Date October 1998

Observer Beth

After observing the child on multiple occasions, describe a favorite activity that the child does often. Add details that you've noticed about the child's interests and choices. Add a photo if you can.

Description:

Every day Brandon heads for the dramatic play area dressing up in costumes which he wears all day when he can. He joins in "cooking" with other children in the kitchen on a regular basis and often suggests ideas and themes for play. Today they are making "spaghetti".

Brandon is on the left

Friends Collection Form

Child's Name Mariah Date 2-8-99
Observer Sharon

Based on your observations, who are this child's friends? What do they do together? How does this child express his or her feelings towards them? Add a photo to illustrate this friendship.

Description:

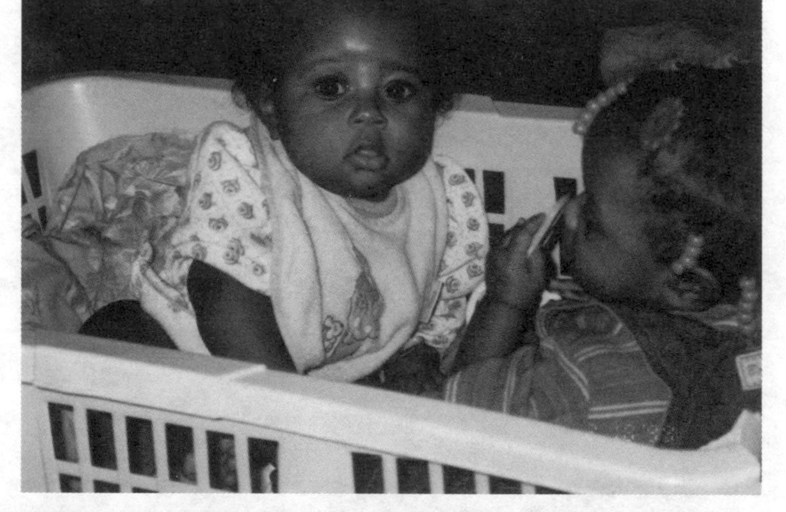

We put Mariah and Katrisse in a basket and let them play unassisted. Mariah reached for Katrisse's barrettes. Katrisse made a noise in protest and Mariah stopped. Mariah latched onto Katrisse's foot and looked at her toes, then at me. She smiled widely.
This type of early awareness of others lays the foundation for future social interactions.

Friends Collection Form

Child's Name Kyle Date October 2, 1998

Observer Kelly

Based on your observations, who are this child's friends? What do they do together? How does this child express his or her feelings towards them? Add a photo to illustrate this friendship.

Description:

Kyle scoots his walker over to play with David almost every day. Today, they got Miss Terry to dress up with them.

"We're cool!" Kyle said.

Family Collection Form

Child's Name Liam Date 10/98

Observer Melissa & Stephen

Families often have stories to share about their child's accomplishments at home. They also have special moments with their child in your classroom. Use this form to document a story that the child's family has shared with you, or take a photo of a special moment between the child and the people who are important in his or her life.

Description:

The attached collage was made by Liam's family in response to a note we sent home requesting a contribution to our "All About Me" bulletin board. (Photos of each child were protected with clear contact paper and then hung on the classroom walls at the toddlers' height.)

Liam frequently points to the various photos and tells the other children and teachers the names of his pets and family members.

Grampy "Bampy" Whitey
Brother Eamon
Liam's house
44 D St.
Liam Loves the beach!
Grandma
"Mymee"
Stella
Liam & Mom
Susan at
the beach
Liam and Dad at Sand Beach
Liam Patrick Kramer-White
"Mean"
"Nana" Pat
Dog-Jasmine
Cat-Possum
Sister
Keshia
27

Family Collection Form

Child's Name Cristina Date 10-24-00
Observer Verónica

Families often have stories to share about their child's accomplishments at home. They also have special moments with their child in your classroom. Use this form to document a story that the child's family has shared with you, or take a photo of a special moment between the child and the people who are important in his or her life.

Description:

Cristina compartió al lado de sus padres y hermanita, en la Noche de las calabazas.

> Documenting Developmental Milestones

Documenting developmental milestones creates a visual record of what each child knows and can do within various areas of development. Anecdotes, photos, and work samples are the pieces of the portfolio that show and explain to family members what the children are accomplishing and how they are progressing.

In the Focused Portfolios™ process, you match the child's everyday work and play in the classroom to well-established developmental expectations. When you pay attention to this match, you raise your professional accountability for what you are doing with the children in your program and the thinking behind your choices of activities, materials, and interactions.

You use the Developmental Milestones Charts in this chapter as a guide so that you know what to expect of infants, toddlers, and preschoolers. You can be much more confident of the work you're doing with the children because you're attuned to watching for development in action. Then you can take photographs, or collect work samples, and write descriptions to show exactly what you've learned about the children in your care.

For young children with special needs, you will be able to easily look across the Developmental Milestones Charts from birth through age five and identify milestones along the continuum that describe each child's strengths, as well as their areas of delay. You can also write Individual Family Service Plans (IFSPs) or Individual Education Plans (IEPs) based on these charts. Your portfolio can then be directly related to these important goals.

Developmental milestones help you plan classroom activities for all of your children. You look carefully at what each child is doing now and refer to the subsequent developmental milestones to determine the next steps to plan for the child. In that way a thoughtful, developmental sequence of activities occurs in your classroom. Developmental milestones help you be sure you are offering appropriate new challenges to each child.

If you are a new teacher, using developmental milestones helps ensure that the fresh activity ideas that you bring to the planning process are grounded in sound developmental theory. You will be guided in what to plan for each age group by referring to the Developmental Milestones Charts, and looking ahead to see which milestones come next for each child.

If you are a seasoned educator with years of experience, using developmental milestones serves as a reminder that your tried and true themes and units, or spontaneous or emergent curriculum projects, must also have a developmental link. You can recheck your favorite activities and make sure they meet the needs of the children in your care right now. You can ask yourself some very important questions:

- "How does each child demonstrate what she knows and can do?"
- "Is my favorite unit or set of activities offering an appropriate degree of challenge while still enabling each child to be successful?"
- "Do I need to make some changes and adaptations for some children?"

When you keep track of children's development by observing them every day and linking your observations to developmental milestones, you'll be able to plan activities that help them progress.

In documenting developmental milestones for infants and toddlers, you will focus on seven areas of development:

- Shows Interest in Others
- Demonstrates Self-Awareness
- Accomplishes Gross-Motor Milestones
- Accomplishes Fine-Motor Milestones
- Communicates
- Acts with Purpose and Uses Tools
- Expresses Feelings

For preschoolers, the age groups are divided into three-year-olds, four-year-olds, and five-year-olds. In documenting developmental milestones for preschoolers, you will focus on seven areas of development:

- Thinking, Reasoning, and Problem Solving
- Emotional and Social Competency
- Language and Communication
- Gross-Motor Development
- Fine-Motor Development
- Reading and Writing Development
- Creative Development

Within each area are specific attitudes, behaviors, and skills that children will demonstrate and that you will document in the portfolio. You will take photographs and write anecdotes that describe what children are doing in relation to these milestones. The full set of Developmental Milestones Charts can be found on the following pages.

Infant/Toddler Developmental Milestones Chart

	Birth to 8 months	8 to 18 months	18 to 24 months	24 months to 3 years
Shows Interest in Others	gazes at others and responds to human voices	exhibits satisfaction in presence of familiar adults	exhibits satisfaction in presence of familiar adults	exhibits satisfaction in presence of familiar adults
	smiles	gets others to do things for own pleasure	shows visible reactions to feelings of others	verbalizes awareness of feelings of others
		shows considerable interest in peers	demonstrates interest in what other children are doing	begins to see benefits of cooperation
				enjoys playing near and with other children
	may show excitement when a familiar adult approaches	is attentive to adult language		enjoys small-group activities
Demonstrates Self-Awareness	observes and plays with own hands	smiles or interacts with self in mirror	shows strong sense of self as individual evidenced by response to name, "No!," "me," and "mine"	uses name of self and others
	tries to cause things to happen	shows awareness of opportunities to make things happen	explores everything	explores everything
	begins to distinguish friends from strangers	identifies one or more body parts	identifies some body parts	labels 6 or more body parts
				makes attempts to self-regulate behavior

Chart continued on next page

Infant/Toddler Developmental Milestones Chart

Accomplishes Gross-Motor Milestones

Birth to 8 months	8 to 18 months	18 to 24 months	24 months to 3 years
lifts head			
holds head up			
rolls over			
sits up unassisted	sits in chairs unassisted		
crawls	pulls self up		
	stands holding furniture		stands on one foot
	walks when led	walks with ease	walks with ease
	walks alone	begins to run	runs easily
	climbs stairs	cautiously walks up and down stairs	walks up and down stairs using alternating feet
	may stoop, trot, and/or walk backwards a few steps	kicks at a ball	kicks a ball
			tiptoes

Chart continued on next page

Infant/Toddler Developmental Milestones Chart

Accomplishes Fine-Motor Milestones

Birth to 8 months	8 to 18 months	18 to 24 months	24 months to 3 years
puts hand or object in mouth	throws objects	threads large beads	threads beads
begins reaching toward interesting objects	feeds self finger food		
reaches and grasps for toys	feeds self partially with fingers and partially with spoon	feeds self with spoon or fork	picks up smaller objects easily
transfers objects hand to hand	uses marker on paper	scribbles with marker or crayon	scribbles with marker or crayon
		imitates a horizontal crayon stroke	draws a circle
		explores scissors	handles scissors with some success

Chart continued on next page

Infant/Toddler Developmental Milestones Chart

Communicates

Birth to 8 months	8 to 18 months	18 to 24 months	24 months to 3 years
smiles or vocalizes to initiate social contact	understands many more words than can say		
babbles to self and others	creates long, babbled sentences		
laughs, listens, and "converses"	shakes head "no"		
understands names of familiar people and objects	says 2 or 3 clear words	combines words in two- and three-word sentences and commands	combines words
	looks at picture books with interest, pointing to objects	listens to short stories (especially one-on-one with an adult)	listens to short stories (one-on-one and in small groups)
	begins to use "me," "you"	labels objects using new vocabulary	speaking vocabulary may reach 200 words
cries to signal pain or distress	uses vocal signals other than crying to gain assistance	begins to play pretend, adding sounds	plays pretend using sounds and words
			uses compound sentences
			recounts events of the day
			uses adjectives and adverbs

Chart continued on next page

Infant/Toddler Developmental Milestones Chart

Acts with Purpose and Uses Tools

Birth to 8 months	8 to 18 months	18 to 24 months	24 months to 3 years
hits at, kicks, shakes, or grasps an object to make a pleasing sight or sound continue	acts to make things happen	explores objects through touch	explores objects through touch
follows a slowly moving object	uses one object (e.g., a stick or a stool) to get another	matches like objects	labels, matches, and sorts objects
looks for a dropped toy	pushes away someone or something not wanted	moves around objects	moves around objects
finds hidden toy when placed while watching	persists in search for hidden toy		
	uses spoon and cup with minimal spilling	uses spoon and cup well	uses feeding utensils well
	tries to build with blocks	stacks rings and blocks, and uses shape sorters	stacks rings and blocks, and uses a variety of manipulative toys
	pushes foot into shoe, arm into sleeve	helps dress and undress self	helps dress and undress self
			puts on garments (cap, slippers)

Chart continued on next page

Infant/Toddler Developmental Milestones Chart

Expresses Feelings

Birth to 8 months	8 to 18 months	18 to 24 months	24 months to 3 years
can usually be comforted by a familiar adult	actively shows affection for familiar person	actively shows affection for familiar person	actively shows affection for familiar person
comforts self	comforts self	is aware of own feelings and those of others	begins to show empathic concern for others
expresses pleasure, joy, excitement, or exuberance	shows pride and pleasure in new accomplishments	shows pride in creation and production	shows pride in creation and production
responds with more animation and pleasure to primary care-giver than to others	shows intense feelings for family members	displays feelings mostly through behavior rather than words	uses words and simple phrases to express some feelings
			expresses emotions with increasing self-control

Preschool Developmental Milestones Chart

Thinking, Reasoning, and Problem Solving

Three-Year-Old Level	Four-Year-Old Level	Five-Year-Old Level
actively explores the world around her	explores the immediate environment and some of the environment beyond home and classroom	demonstrates interest in exploring aspects of home, school, and community
engages in make-believe play, and imitates adult roles, responsibilities, and phenomena in his or her life	uses increasingly complex dramatic play to clarify roles, relationships, and responsibilities of self and others	uses complex, planned, and scripted dramatic play, often involving many children in the discussion and negotiation of roles
uses one object to stand for another in dramatic play ("This broom is the firehose.")	uses a variety of objects to represent other objects in dramatic play	experiments with a wide variety of materials to find challenging new ways to utilize and combine them
focuses on the observable and tangible aspects of objects and events	focuses on the observable and tangible aspects of objects and events	
approaches new tasks and solves problems through observation, hands-on trial and error, and repetition	begins to generate ideas and suggestions, and makes plans and predictions when asked	sustains interest in a task, and works hard to solve problems independently, or with some adult coaching and support
matches identical items and pictures	groups objects using 2 or more attributes (e.g., by size and color)	groups items into higher order categories and classes of objects
sorts objects into simple categories	verbalizes own interpretations of cause and effect when solving problems	
counts objects, but does not yet have one-to-one correspondence	counts objects with emerging one-to-one correspondence	counts objects, and refers to the quantity of items in talking about them, often one-to-one correspondence
		uses measurement words (e.g., longer, shorter, heavier, lighter) and tools (e.g., rulers, measuring tapes, Unifix cubes, and balance scales) *Chart continued on next page*

Preschool Developmental Milestones Chart

Emotional & Social Competency

Three-Year-Old Level	Four-Year-Old Level	Five-Year-Old Level
plays alone or alongside others, sometimes copying others, or following their suggestions	still plays alongside others, but is beginning to play cooperatively, as "being friends" becomes increasingly important	plays with "best friends" extensively
asserts own needs and wants, and is beginning to negotiate conflict with peers	begins to willingly take turns, mostly to ensure that others will "be friends"	cooperates most of the time in group play and work time
expresses intense feelings, such as affection or joy	works hard to use language to express feelings, negotiate, and resolve disagreements, with adult help	uses language to express feelings, negotiate, and resolve disagreements, with minimal adult intervention
becoming comfortable separating from familiar adults	over time, shows comfort with new people and situations	over time shows comfort with new people and situations
may sense another's feelings and show empathy	begins to spontaneously offer help, comfort, or objects to others	can sense another person's feelings, and has some ideas about how to help others
achieves some independence with routine tasks such as dressing self, using the bathroom, and cleaning up after playing or eating	manages routines such as dressing self, using the bathroom, and cleaning up after play, snacks, or meals, often independently	manages routines such as dressing self, using the bathroom, and cleaning up after play, snacks, or meals, mostly independently
	is beginning to comprehend that there are consequences to one's actions	is beginning to understand the consequences of own and others' behavior

Chart continued on next page

Preschool Developmental Milestones Chart

	Three-Year-Old Level	Four-Year-Old Level	Five-Year-Old Level
Language & Communication	vocabulary increasing steadily, using sentences of at least 3 or 4 words to express wants and needs	talks to others about personal acquaintances, experiences, and acquisitions (in small and large groups)	uses complex sentence structure, and has the vocabulary to express most wants, needs, and explanations, without difficulty
	begins to listen and attend to others	listens to others and tries to participate in conversation	participates actively in conversations, listening attentively and with patience to others' contributions
	learns words to simple finger plays, rhymes, and songs, especially those with a lot of repetition and hand motions	restates multi-step directions	can follow multi-step instructions and requests
	can tell a simple story, often focusing only on favorite parts	can retell the basic sequence of a story	remembers and recites poems, songs, and story and movie sequences, and acts them out
		uses some positional words (e.g., under, over, on)	uses positional words (e.g., under, over, on)
Gross-Motor Development	walks, runs, turns, and stops well	walks, runs, turns, and stops well	skips and runs with agility and speed
	is developing coordination in a variety of situations	beginning to skip	coordinates movements for swimming, skating, or bike riding
	balances with emerging skill	can balance and climb in many situations	balances, hops, jumps, and climbs well
	plays actively and then needs rest	exhibits increasing physical endurance	displays high energy level

Chart continued on next page

Preschool Developmental Milestones Chart

Fine-Motor Development

Three-Year-Old Level	Four-Year-Old Level	Five-Year-Old Level
manipulates large pegs, beads, and puzzles with knobs, or whole pieces representing objects	uses puzzles with small pieces, small pegs, beads, playdough, eyedroppers, etc.	does multiple-piece puzzles, and uses small manipulatives with ease
pours liquids with some spills	pours sand or liquids into small containers	
builds simple block structures	builds complex block structures	builds 3-dimensional block structures
holds crayon or marker in fingers instead of fist	draws combinations of shapes and objects that are recognizable to adults	draws persons and geometric designs
draws shapes and objects in some relation to each other	draws persons with at least 4 parts	prints first name and prints some letters crudely but readably for adults
handles scissors with some success	uses scissors with increasing skill	uses hammers, scissors, screwdrivers, and hole punchers unassisted
dresses and undresses with some assistance	dresses and undresses without assistance	dresses and undresses easily, tying shoes with adult coaching

Chart continued on next page

Preschool Developmental Milestones Chart

Reading & Writing Development

Three-Year-Old Level	Four-Year-Old Level	Five-Year-Old Level
is curious about print in the environment	"reads" some print in the environment (names, letters, signs, labels, logos)	"reads" print in the environment (many classmates' names, alphabet letters, "Exit" and restroom signs, labels, logos)
may play at reading by reading the pictures	plays at reading by reading the pictures	role-plays self as reader, relying heavily on memory, pictures, and/or some word recognition
listens to stories read aloud, asks questions	listens to stories read aloud, asks questions, and makes pertinent comments	listens to stories read aloud, and discusses plot and characters
	is curious about letters, words, and some conventions of print (front-to-back, directionality of books)	is curious about letters, words, and conventions of print, and may ask how to spell words
plays at writing, and may combine writing and drawing	plays at writing using scribbles, random symbols and letters, and some conventional words and names	writes using scribbles, random symbols and letters, and conventional words and names

Chart continued on next page

Preschool Developmental Milestones Chart

Creative Development

Three-Year-Old Level	Four-Year-Old Level	Five-Year-Old Level
attempts to use various tools to express self through random marks, drawings, paintings, or building	uses various tools with increasing control to express self through designs, drawings, paintings, or building	regularly uses various tools with control to express self through designs, drawings, paintings, or building
may begin to name a person, place, thing, or action in a drawing	sometimes names a person, place, thing, or action in a drawing	sometimes names a person, place, thing, or action in a drawing
		includes detail in drawings and artwork
responds to music through spontaneous body movements	responds to music through rhythmic body movements	responds to music through rhythmic, controlled body movements
engages in pretend play	engages in pretend play easily and naturally	engages in dramatic play easily, cooperating with other children, and showing lots of imagination and interest
explores the uses and properties of expressive media (paint, chalk, crayon, pencils, clay, collage materials, wood, etc.)	explores a variety of expressive media (paint, chalk, crayon, pencils, clay, collage materials, wood, etc.)	explores a variety of expressive media with purpose, often with a product in mind (paint, chalk, crayon, pencils, clay, collage materials, wood, etc.)

> The Continuum of Development

The celebration of children's ongoing development and accomplishment gives the portfolio a very positive tone. The message to families is that learning and development are continuous. If children have not yet achieved particular skills, or acquired various concepts, they will. Time and maturation, combined with more experiences and nurturing adults, will support growth and learning. The manner in which the Developmental Milestones Charts are laid out helps teachers and families to see the continuous, step-by-step patterns in each area of development.

We have formatted the charts so that you can look across the age span for each area of development on the page. That way, you can see very clearly the continuum of developmental expectations. You will also be able to see how your observations of some children's performance will cross the boundaries of differing ages.

When teachers observe a group of children within the same age range, they notice that no two children are exactly the same in all areas of development. They use the continuum of development to pinpoint each child's unique picture of accomplishment.

For example, look at Accomplishes Gross-Motor Milestones for ages eight months to eighteen months on the Developmental Milestones Charts. You can see that only some children will be walking alone or climbing stairs. Some will still be standing and holding onto furniture, or walking only when led. Clearly, children within this age range are all accomplishing different milestones. Your documentation will note exactly what each child can do, what she routinely does, and celebrate her accomplishments.

You may have an eighteen-month-old who performs fine-motor tasks in the eight- to eighteen-month-old range, but whose language abilities are in the eighteen- to twenty-four-month range. You may have a thirty-two-month-old whose interest in others is more characteristic of an earlier age level, while her use of tools for a purpose is far more advanced. A four-year-old may perform fine-motor tasks in the three-year-old level, but have the language abilities of a five-year-old. A five-year-old may have emotional and social competencies of an earlier age level, while his thinking, reasoning, and problem solving are far more advanced. These are normal developmental portraits of growing children. For all children, there are areas of development in which they are advancing rapidly, and areas in which they are slower at becoming competent.

Sometimes you'll have a photo and anecdote that shows milestone achievement and is also a Friends, Family, or Favorites item. For example, in documenting milestones about Shows Interest in Others for infants and toddlers, or Emotional and Social Competency for preschoolers, the photo and anecdote may portray the child playing with best friends. The portfolio will be integrated with many overlapping items to provide information about the whole child.

All teachers should certainly take time to study the Developmental Milestones Charts for the age group they teach and become familiar with their contents. Obviously, a preschool teacher will focus more intently on learning the preschool charts, while a teacher of infants and toddlers will focus on the ones for that age group. Teachers of young children with special needs will benefit from looking across the full continuum. This is also true for teachers working in settings with typically developing young children. For example, if you work with older toddlers, you will want to pay attention to the preschool three-year-old level charts so that you can recognize areas in which your two-and-a-half-year-olds are advanced. While those who teach three-year-olds may want to refer back to the older toddler levels.

Take some time to study these charts and become familiar with their contents. They are your resource and guide as you begin the process of collecting documentation for the portfolios.

> Developmental Milestones Collection Forms

Special collection forms have been designed for documenting developmental milestones for infants and toddlers and for preschoolers. Version #1 is designed for teachers using the Developmental Milestones Charts in this book. Version #2 is designed for programs using their own favorite developmental charts. Version #3 is designed to tie directly to IFSP and IEP goals for young children with special needs. The three types of forms appear on the following pages. *(All three versions of the forms, ready for you to photocopy, can be found in appendix A.)* You will see completed samples of these three forms later in this chapter.

Developmental Milestones Collection Form
Version #1 Infant/Toddler

Child's Name ______________________________ Age __________

Observer ______________________________ Date __________

Check off the *areas of development* that apply:

- ❑ Shows interest in others
- ❑ Demonstrates self-awareness
- ❑ Accomplishes gross-motor milestones
- ❑ Accomplishes fine-motor milestones
- ❑ Communicates
- ❑ Acts with purpose and uses tools
- ❑ Expresses feelings

This photo, work sample and/or anecdote illustrates the following *developmental milestone(s):*

____

____

____

____

Check off whatever applies to the context of this observation:

- ❑ Child-initiated activity
- ❑ Teacher-initiated activity
- ❑ New task for this child
- ❑ Familiar task for this child
- ❑ Done independently
- ❑ Done with adult guidance
- ❑ Done with peer(s)
- ❑ Time spent (1–5 mins.)
- ❑ Time spent (5–15 mins.)
- ❑ Time spent (15+ mins.)

Anecdotal Note: Describe what you saw the child do and/or heard the child say.

Developmental Milestones Collection Form
Version #1 Preschooler

Child's Name ______________________ Age __________

Observer ______________________ Date __________

Check off the *areas of development* that apply:

- ❏ Thinking, Reasoning & Problem-Solving
- ❏ Emotional and Social Competency
- ❏ Gross-Motor Development
- ❏ Fine-Motor Development
- ❏ Language and Communication
- ❏ Reading & Writing Development
- ❏ Creative Development

This photo, work sample and/or anecdote illustrates the following *developmental milestone(s):*

____

____

____

____

Check off whatever applies to the context of this observation:

- ❏ Child-initiated activity
- ❏ Teacher-initiated activity
- ❏ New task for this child
- ❏ Familiar task for this child
- ❏ Done independently
- ❏ Done with adult guidance
- ❏ Done with peer(s)
- ❏ Time spent (1–5 mins.)
- ❏ Time spent (5–15 mins.)
- ❏ Time spent (15+ mins.)

Anecdotal Note: Describe what you saw the child do and/or heard the child say.

Developmental Milestones Collection Form
Version #2 Infant/Toddler
(using your own developmental charts)

Child's Name ______________________ Age __________

Observer ______________________ Date __________

List the *areas of development* that apply:

____

____

____

This photo, work sample and/or anecdote illustrates the following *developmental milestone(s):*

____

____

____

Check off whatever applies to the context of this observation:

- ❑ Child-initiated activity
- ❑ Teacher-initiated activity
- ❑ New task for this child
- ❑ Familiar task for this child
- ❑ Done independently
- ❑ Done with adult guidance
- ❑ Done with peer(s)
- ❑ Time spent (1–5 mins.)
- ❑ Time spent (5–15 mins.)
- ❑ Time spent (15+ mins.)

Anecdotal Note: Describe what you saw the child do and/or heard the child say.

Developmental Milestones Collection Form
Version #2 Preschooler
(using your own developmental charts)

Child's Name ______________________________ Age ____________

Observer ______________________________ Date ____________

List the *areas of development* that apply:

____

____

____

This photo, work sample and/or anecdote illustrates the following *developmental milestone(s):*

____

____

____

Check off whatever applies to the context of this observation:

- ❑ Child-initiated activity
- ❑ Teacher-initiated activity
- ❑ New task for this child
- ❑ Familiar task for this child
- ❑ Done independently
- ❑ Done with adult guidance
- ❑ Done with peer(s)
- ❑ Time spent (1–5 mins.)
- ❑ Time spent (5–15 mins.)
- ❑ Time spent (15+ mins.)

Anecdotal Note: Describe what you saw the child do and/or heard the child say.

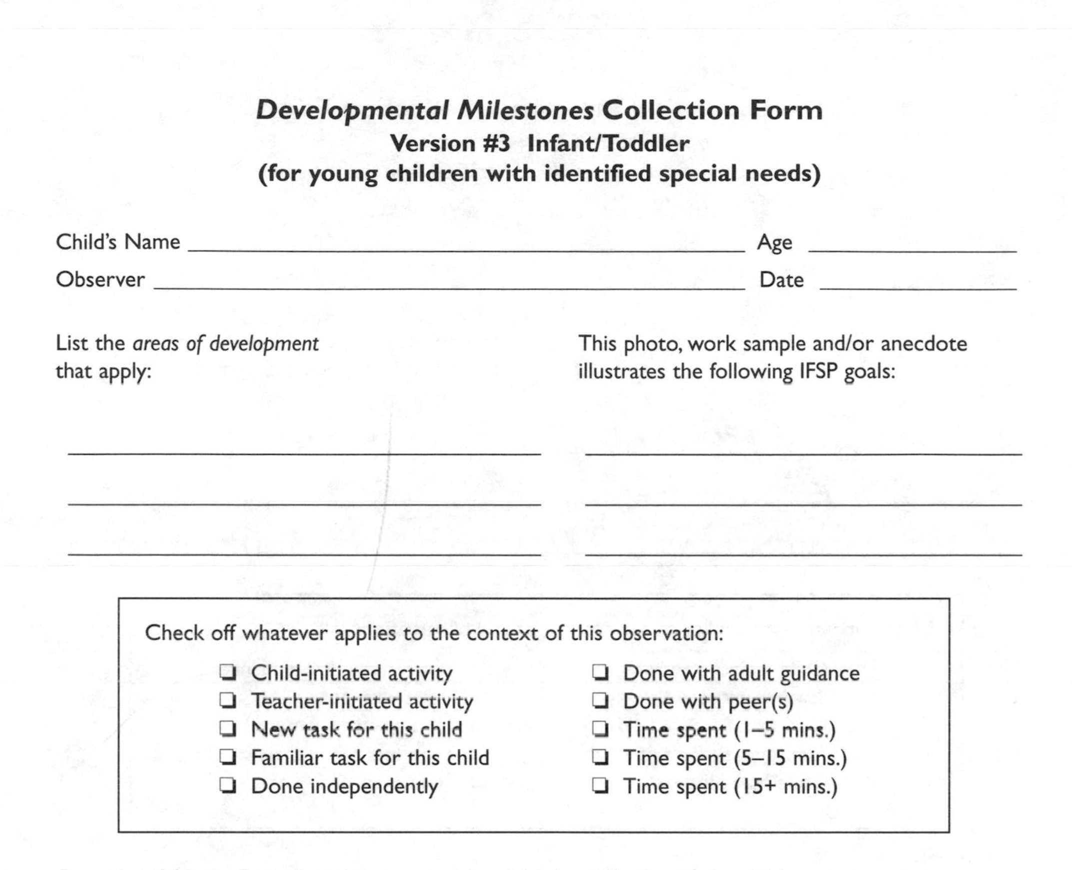

Developmental Milestones Collection Form
Version #3 Infant/Toddler
(for young children with identified special needs)

Child's Name ______________________________ Age __________

Observer ______________________________ Date __________

List the *areas of development* that apply:

____

____

____

This photo, work sample and/or anecdote illustrates the following IFSP goals:

____

____

____

Check off whatever applies to the context of this observation:

- ❏ Child-initiated activity
- ❏ Teacher-initiated activity
- ❏ New task for this child
- ❏ Familiar task for this child
- ❏ Done independently
- ❏ Done with adult guidance
- ❏ Done with peer(s)
- ❏ Time spent (1–5 mins.)
- ❏ Time spent (5–15 mins.)
- ❏ Time spent (15+ mins.)

Anecdotal Note: Describe what you saw the child do and/or heard the child say.

Developmental Milestones Collection Form
Version #3 Preschooler
(for young children with identified special needs)

Child's Name ______________________________ Age ____________

Observer ______________________________ Date ____________

List the *areas of development* that apply:

____

____

____

This photo, work sample and/or anecdote illustrates the following IEP goals:

____

____

____

Check off whatever applies to the context of this observation:

- ❑ Child-initiated activity
- ❑ Teacher-initiated activity
- ❑ New task for this child
- ❑ Familiar task for this child
- ❑ Done independently
- ❑ Done with adult guidance
- ❑ Done with peer(s)
- ❑ Time spent (1–5 mins.)
- ❑ Time spent (5–15 mins.)
- ❑ Time spent (15+ mins.)

Anecdotal Note: Describe what you saw the child do and/or heard the child say.

Similar to the collection forms for Favorites, Friends, and Family, these milestones forms include spaces for the child's name, age at the time of observation, the date of the observation, and your name as the observer.

Below this information on the left-hand side of the form is the list of the areas of development from the milestones charts. The list for infants and toddlers will differ from that used for preschoolers. Place a check mark next to the primary (most evident) area of development that you observe. If you are just beginning with this process, we recommend that you check off only one area of development on each collection form. See Linsey's sample collection in chapter 3 for this basic approach. If you are ready to add more complexity to the collection process, you can check off more than one area of development on each of the seven forms. See details on how to do this and examples of this approach in Sierra's collection in chapter 6.

Next, on the blank lines provided on the right-hand side of the form, list the specific developmental milestone(s) that describe the attitudes, behaviors, or skills that the anecdote, photo, or work sample is documenting. These milestones can be found right on the Developmental Milestones Charts. For more direction and ideas about how and when to write these milestones on the form, refer to the section titled "Two Ways to Collect Documentation" in chapter 4.

Documenting the Context of the Observation

The Developmental Milestones Collection Forms include a very quick and easy way for you to note how the child went about accomplishing the task you were observing. Notice the checklist in the box on the collection form. There are several choices for you to check off:

- Did the child initiate the activity?
- Or did the teacher?
- Was this a new task for the child?
- Or a familiar one?
- How long a period of time was the child involved in the activity?

This checklist adds important details that you have witnessed. By noting the length of time the child was involved in the activity, or the degree of independence you observed, you are documenting the context in which the observation took place. Then, when you review your notes at a later date, you'll be able to remember exactly how the child went about completing the task at hand. And, when you share the form with families or other teachers, they too will have that important information.

Next on the Developmental Milestones Collection Form is a space for your description or anecdotal note. Here, in simple, straightforward phrases, you describe what you saw the child do and/or heard the child say. For example, "Today, Benjamin climbed up the steps of the small slide all by himself. When he reached the top, he turned around, looked at me, and smiled broadly." This anecdote is factual, not judgmental, and tells more of the story in addition to the check marks that you made about how the child went about the task.

Finally on the form is a space in which to paste a photograph (if you have one). If you have a work sample instead, simply staple the collection form to the child's work and write the words "Work Sample Attached" so others will know to refer to the next page.

When Your Anecdote Is Lengthy

As you did with the collection of items for the Favorites, Friends, and Family categories, use the Focused Portfolios™ Photo Form when you have written a particularly lengthy anecdote on the Developmental Milestones Collection Form and need an additional page to attach the photograph. Simply staple the photo form to the Developmental Milestones Collection Form, and your documentation is ready to file.

Matching Documentation to Areas of Development

The areas of development for infants and toddlers lend themselves most easily to documentation through photographs and anecdotes. Some of the areas of development for preschoolers are more effectively demonstrated through actual work samples produced by the children. Sometimes videotape or audiotape can be effective in documenting children's development. If you have the equipment and the ability to use it, you may choose to tape-record children's actual words, or videotape their dramatic play or gross-motor accomplishments. You make the decision based on your own preferences and resources.

Recommended types of documentation for infants, toddlers, and preschoolers appear in the tables on the following two pages.

Recommended Types of Documentation for Infants and Toddlers

Area of Development	Recommended Types of Documentation
Shows interest in others	Photographs with anecdotes (such as babies playing near each other, in high chairs grouped together, or with adults; a toddler playing "peek-a-boo"), or stand-alone anecdotes
Demonstrates self-awareness	Photographs with anecdotes (such as mirror play; touching and labeling body parts during finger plays and songs; babies causing a toy to make a noise), or stand-alone anecdotes
Accomplishes gross-motor milestones	Photographs with anecdotes (such as babies kicking feet or swinging hands to move mobiles or crib gyms; toddlers using pull/push toys), stand-alone anecdotes, or videotape
Accomplishes fine-motor milestones	Photographs with anecdotes (such as child playing with busy box or crib toys, rattles, or playdough), stand-alone anecdotes, work sample of scribbles, or fingerpainting on paper
Communicates	Direct quotes of children's language on Infant/Toddler Word List *(see appendix A)*, audiotape or videotape, photographs with anecdotes or stand-alone anecdotes
Acts with purpose and uses tools	Photographs with anecdotes (such as toddler using a rolling pin or Popsicle sticks with dough; infant using a spoon; toddler pushing a stool to the sink), stand-alone anecdotes, or work samples (for example, gluing or painting samples)
Expresses feelings	Photographs with anecdotes (such as clapping hands to show delight; loudly saying "No!" when a peer takes away a toy), or stand-alone anecdotes

Recommended Types of Documentation for Preschoolers

Area of Development	Recommended Types of Documentation
Thinking, Reasoning, and Problem Solving	Photographs with anecdotes (such as children engaged in block construction, puzzle making, work with manipulative toys, sand and water play, experiments with objects); work samples, including paintings or drawings that incorporate shapes, sorting, or counting, accompanied by anecdotes with the children's explanations; child-produced number books, with anecdotes; written scripts or videotape of spontaneous dramatic play accompanied by anecdotes; written quotes of child's problem solving or use of imagination, or audiotapes of the same; or stand-alone anecdotes
Emotional and Social Competency	Photographs with anecdotes; or stand-alone anecdotes (such as descriptions of children working through conflicts with peers)
Language and Communication	Direct quotes of children's language accompanied by anecdotes; audiotape or videotape with anecdotes; photographs with anecdotes, or stand-alone anecdotes
Gross-Motor Development	Photographs with anecdotes; videotape with anecdotes (such as children playing outdoors, in block play, or music and movement); or stand-alone anecdotes
Fine-Motor Development	Work samples (of drawings, writing, or cutting) with anecdotes; photographs with anecdotes (such as work with manipulative toys, weaving, gluing/collage, clay, and dough); or stand-alone anecdotes
Reading and Writing Development	Work samples of children's writing, with anecdotes; book lists of favorite books to be read at home and school, with anecdotes; teacher-written dictations, or anecdotes to accompany audiotapes of child retelling a familiar story; videotape of child "reading" favorite story from memory; illustrations, drawings, or paintings relating to stories read aloud, with anecdotes; anecdote capturing child's puppet play; photographs with anecdotes; or stand-alone anecdotes
Creative Development	Work samples of drawings and paintings, with anecdotes; videotape or photographs of child dancing to music, playing instruments, or dramatizing, accompanied by anecdotes; photographs with anecdotes (clay, dough, collage, or other media); or stand-alone anecdotes

> Examples of Developmental Milestones Collection Forms

Here are some completed examples of all three versions of the Developmental Milestones Collection Forms. All of the examples use the basic approach of documenting one area of development at a time. Read the anecdotes carefully. Look at the different ways teachers document these important parts of children's development. Think about your children's accomplishments, growing skills and behaviors, their changing development. How will you be documenting these in your program?

Developmental Milestones Collection Form
Version #1 Infant/Toddler

Child's Name Andrea Age 2 yrs. 2 mos.
Observer Sara Date April 6, 1999

Check off the *areas of development* that apply:

- ☐ Shows interest in others
- ☐ Demonstrates self-awareness
- ☐ Accomplishes gross-motor milestones
- ☑ Accomplishes fine-motor milestones
- ☐ Communicates
- ☐ Acts with purpose and uses tools
- ☐ Expresses feelings

This photo, work sample and/or anecdote illustrates the following *developmental milestone(s):*

scribbles with marker or crayon; imitates a horizontal crayon stroke

Check off whatever applies to the context of this observation:

- ☐ Child-initiated activity
- ☑ Teacher-initiated activity
- ☐ New task for this child
- ☑ Familiar task for this child
- ☑ Done independently
- ☐ Done with adult guidance
- ☐ Done with peer(s)
- ☐ Time spent (1-5 mins.)
- ☑ Time spent (5-15 mins.)
- ☐ Time spent (15+ mins.)

Anecdotal Note: Describe what you saw the child do and/or heard the child say.

Today, Andrea drew a variety of shapes. Note that almost every circle drawn was a closed shape. She scribbled a separate black line across the top and told me it was her name.

(See attached work sample)

My name

Developmental Milestones Collection Form
Version #1 Infant/Toddler

Child's Name Malik Age 10 months
Observer Sharon Date 12/98

Check off the *areas of development* that apply:

- ☐ Shows interest in others
- ☒ Demonstrates self-awareness
- ☐ Accomplishes gross-motor milestones
- ☐ Accomplishes fine-motor milestones
- ☐ Communicates
- ☐ Acts with purpose and uses tools
- ☐ Expresses feelings

This photo, work sample and/or anecdote illustrates the following *developmental milestone(s):*

shows awareness of opportunities to make things happen

Check off whatever applies to the context of this observation:

☒ Child-initiated activity	☐ Done with adult guidance
☐ Teacher-initiated activity	☐ Done with peer(s)
☒ New task for this child	☐ Time spent (1-5 mins.)
☐ Familiar task for this child	☒ Time spent (5-15 mins.)
☒ Done independently	☐ Time spent (15+ mins.)

Anecdotal Note: Describe what you saw the child do and/or heard the child say.

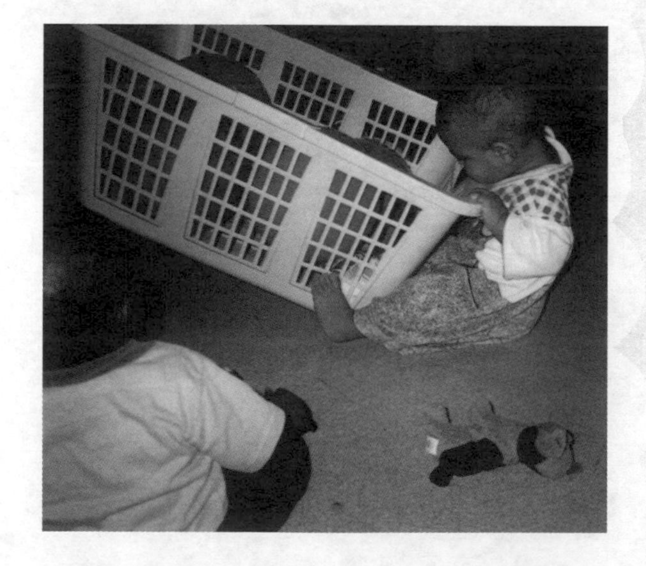

Malik couldn't reach the ball he wanted when standing up over the basket. So, he sat down and pulled the basket up to reach it!

Developmental Milestones Collection Form
Version #1 Preschooler

Child's Name Nicholas Age 4
Observer Maria Date 4/16/99

Check off the *areas of development* that apply:

- ❑ Thinking, Reasoning & Problem-Solving
- ☑ Emotional and Social Competency
- ❑ Gross-Motor Development
- ❑ Fine-Motor Development
- ❑ Language and Communication
- ❑ Reading & Writing Development
- ❑ Creative Development

This photo, work sample and/or anecdote illustrates the following *developmental milestone(s):*

can sense a person's feelings and has some ideas how to help.

Check off whatever applies to the context of this observation:

- ☑ Child-initiated activity
- ❑ Teacher-initiated activity
- ❑ New task for this child
- ☑ Familiar task for this child
- ❑ Done independently
- ❑ Done with adult guidance
- ☑ Done with peer(s)
- ☑ Time spent (1-5 mins.)
- ❑ Time spent (5-15 mins.)
- ❑ Time spent (15+ mins.)

Anecdotal Note: Describe what you saw the child do and/or heard the child say.

Jessica and Darianne were fighting over the dolls. Nicholas saw them fighting. He picked up the extra doll and tried to hand it to Darianne. I heard him say "Darianne you can have this one."

Developmental Milestones Collection Form
Version #1 Preschooler

Child's Name BETH ANNE Age 5
Observer LORA Date 3/24/99

Check off the *areas of development* that apply:

- ❑ Thinking, Reasoning & Problem-Solving
- ❑ Emotional and Social Competency
- ❑ Gross-Motor Development
- ❑ Fine-Motor Development
- ❑ Language and Communication
- ❑ Reading & Writing Development
- ☒ Creative Development

This photo, work sample and/or anecdote illustrates the following *developmental milestone(s):*

SOMETIMES NAMES A PERSON, PLACE OR THING IN A DRAWING; INCLUDES DETAIL IN DRAWINGS AND ARTWORK

Check off whatever applies to the context of this observation:

- ❑ Child-initiated activity
- ☒ Teacher-initiated activity
- ❑ New task for this child
- ☒ Familiar task for this child
- ☒ Done independently
- ❑ Done with adult guidance
- ❑ Done with peer(s)
- ☒ Time spent (1-5 mins.)
- ❑ Time spent (5-15 mins.)
- ❑ Time spent (15+ mins.)

Anecdotal Note: Describe what you saw the child do and/or heard the child say.

BETH ANNE SAID THAT SHE WAS DRAWING HERSELF WITH "CRAZY HAIR" AND TEETH!

Beth Anne

Developmental Milestones Collection Form
Version #1 Preschooler

Child's Name Grant Age 5.1
Observer Camille Date 1-18-00

Check off the *areas of development* that apply:

- [x] Thinking, Reasoning & Problem-Solving
- [ ] Emotional and Social Competency
- [ ] Gross-Motor Development
- [ ] Fine-Motor Development
- [ ] Language and Communication
- [ ] Reading & Writing Development
- [ ] Creative Development

This photo, work sample and/or anecdote illustrates the following *developmental milestone(s):*

* Experiments with a wide variety of materials

Check off whatever applies to the context of this observation:

- [x] Child-initiated activity
- [ ] Teacher-initiated activity
- [x] New task for this child
- [ ] Familiar task for this child
- [ ] Done independently
- [ ] Done with adult guidance
- [ ] Done with peer(s)
- [ ] Time spent (1-5 mins.)
- [x] Time spent (5-15 mins.)
- [ ] Time spent (15+ mins.)

Anecdotal Note: Describe what you saw the child do and/or heard the child say.

Grant stayed for a long time at the sensory table where we had shredded toilet paper, dish soap and water. He explored the material and put it over his hands, lifting it up and watching it "plop" back down, with a big smile on his face.

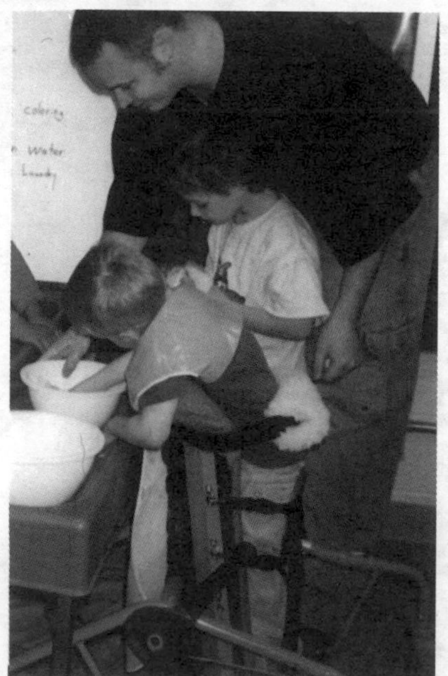

Developmental Milestones Collection Form
Version #2 Infant/Toddler
(using your own developmental charts)

Child's Name Charisse Age 20 months
Observer Barb Date 3-17-99

List the *areas of development* that apply:

Using AEPS (Bricker)
Adaptive Domain: Feeding

This photo, work sample and/or anecdote illustrates the following *developmental milestone(s):*

brings food to mouth with intensil.

Check off whatever applies to the context of this observation:

- [x] Child-initiated activity
- [ ] Teacher-initiated activity
- [x] New task for this child
- [ ] Familiar task for this child
- [x] Done independently
- [ ] Done with adult guidance
- [ ] Done with peer(s)
- [ ] Time spent (1-5 mins.)
- [x] Time spent (5-15 mins.)
- [ ] Time spent (15+ mins.)

Anecdotal Note: Describe what you saw the child do and/or heard the child say.

We have been encouraging Charisse to use a spoon at meal-time. Today, she was quite successful and spilled very little!

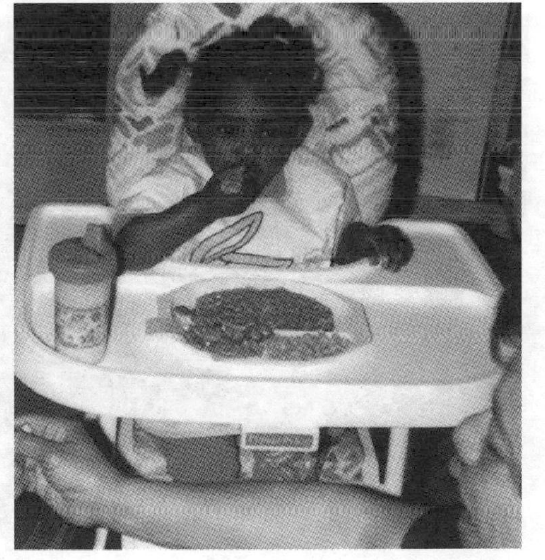

Developmental Milestones Collection Form
Version #2 Infant/Toddler
(using your own developmental charts)

Child's Name Shannon Age 2 yrs, 8 mos.
Observer Carol Date 7/12/98

List the *areas of development* that apply:

Using High/Scope® Child Observation Record

Logic and Mathematics: Using comparison words

This photo, work sample and/or anecdote illustrates the following *developmental milestone(s)*:

Child follows directions that involve comparison words.

Check off whatever applies to the context of this observation:

- ☐ Child-initiated activity
- ☑ Teacher-initiated activity
- ☑ New task for this child
- ☐ Familiar task for this child
- ☐ Done independently
- ☑ Done with adult guidance
- ☐ Done with peer(s)
- ☐ Time spent (1-5 mins.)
- ☑ Time spent (5-15 mins.)
- ☐ Time spent (15+ mins.)

Anecdotal Note: Describe what you saw the child do and/or heard the child say.

I asked Shannon to pour the grated zucchini from the smaller cup into the larger bowl. She said "That's a big bowl!" She helped grate the zucchini, and had also helped harvest it from our garden earlier in the day.

Developmental Milestones Collection Form
Version #3 Preschooler
(For young children with identified special needs)

Child's Name Grant Age 4.11 yrs.
Observer Camille Date 11-14-99

List the *areas of development* that apply:

Communication

This photo, work sample and/or anecdote illustrates the following IEP goals:

tries to participate in conversations (in American Sign Language)

Check off whatever applies to the context of this observation:

- [x] Child-initiated activity
- [ ] Teacher-initiated activity
- [ ] New task for this child
- [x] Familiar task for this child
- [x] Done independently
- [ ] Done with adult guidance
- [ ] Done with peer(s)
- [ ] Time spent (1-5 mins.)
- [x] Time spent (5-15 mins.)
- [ ] Time spent (15+ mins.)

Anecdotal Note: Describe what you saw the child do and/or heard the child say.

As Emma, Sarah and Brett approached Grant as they waited to go outside, they noticed that he did not have his shoes on. Brett sat in a chair at Grant's eye level and gently tapped his shoulder to get Grant's attention. Grant turned his head. In sign, Brett asked Grant, "Do you want to go outside?" Grant responded, "Outside." Brett asked, "Yes, outside?" Grant responded with a big smile, "Yes, outside." Brett said, "Fine. Where are your shoes?" Grant, looking surprised, said, "My shoes are gone. Shoes are over there." Emma got his shoes and brought them to Grant. With a big smile Grant said, "Thank you." Emma and Brett helped put his shoes on.

***Developmental Milestones* Collection Form**
Version #3 Preschooler
(For young children with identified special needs)

Child's Name Austin Age 4. 6
Observer Anji Date 10-30-00

List the *areas of development* that apply:

Cognitive

This photo, work sample and/or anecdote illustrates the following IEP goals:

Austin will give a requested object to a peer/adult when presented in a field of 3 with a prompt at the wrist

Check off whatever applies to the context of this observation:

- ❑ Child-initiated activity
- ☒ Teacher-initiated activity
- ❑ New task for this child
- ❑ Familiar task for this child
- ❑ Done independently
- ☒ Done with adult guidance
- ❑ Done with peer(s)
- ❑ Time spent (1-5 mins.)
- ❑ Time spent (5-15 mins.)
- ❑ Time spent (15+ mins.)

Anecdotal Note: Describe what you saw the child do and/or heard the child say.

Austin gave me the weather board by holding it with 2 hands and extending his arms toward me when given the direction "Give it to Mrs. Anji."
In the past Austin has needed hand over hand assistance in order to locate a labeled object in a field of more than 1.

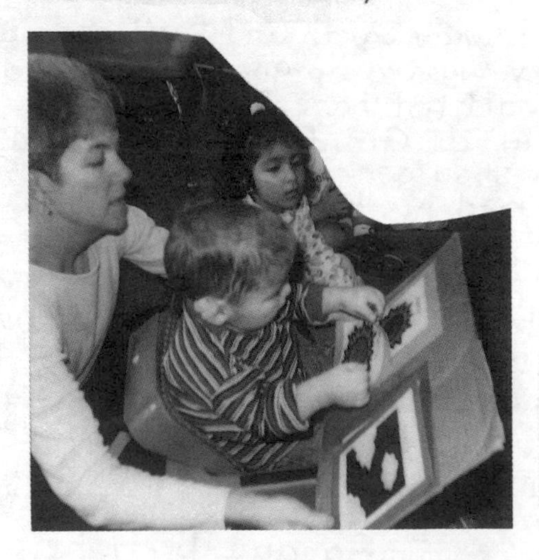

chapter 3

Favorites Collection Form
Child's Name Brandon
Observer Beth
Date October 1998

> A Basic Portfolio: Linsey

Linsey's teacher, Beth Hendricks, collected the following ten items for Linsey's portfolio after receiving training in the Focused Portfolios™ process. This was her first attempt at portfolio collection, although she was used to taking lots of photographs and putting them together in a slide show to present to families at the end of the year. Beth used the basic approach of identifying and checking off one area of development for each Developmental Milestones Collection Form. This helped her learn through practice the observation and documentation approach presented in this book. We agree that this is a good way to start.

Look through this collection and note the way the forms are filled out. Read the anecdotes and look at the photographs. Check out the milestones identified and match them with the descriptions of Linsey's actions. We recommend that you use this collection as a learning tool before you begin collecting portfolio items.

We are grateful to Beth, and to Linsey and her family, for sharing with us. They have given teachers a valuable resource.

Favorites Collection Form

Child's Name Linsey Date 12-98

Observer Beth

After observing the child on multiple occasions, describe a favorite activity that the child does often. Add details that you've noticed about the child's interests and choices. Add a photo if you can.

Description: Linsey often paints and explores the many different paint brushes, every day if they're available. Today, she painted and painted with a medium-size brush, mixing colors and commenting on them.

Other favorite activities that Linsey often chooses include blocks, dress-up, animals and puzzles.

Friends Collection Form

Child's Name Linsey Date 11-98

Observer Beth

Based on your observations, who are this child's friends? What do they do together? How does this child express his or her feelings towards them? Add a photo to illustrate this friendship.

Description: Linsey is usually on her own – deeply involved in her chosen activity. But if she chooses to play with others, Brandon is one friend she chooses to join. Here, she is "very sick" and in need of some medical assistance – STAT! Thanks Doctor Brandon!

Family Collection Form

Child's Name Linsey Date 12-16-98

Observer Beth

Families often have stories to share about their child's accomplishments at home. They also have special moments with their child in your classroom. Use this form to document a story that the child's family has shared with you, or take a photo of a special moment between the child and the people who are important in his or her life.

Description: Here, Mom and Linsey build a zoo with the blocks and animals. Linsey often plays with the animals in the block area. Whenever Mom comes to help in the classroom, Linsey stays close by and asks her Mom to play with her in different areas.

Developmental Milestones Collection Form
Version #1 Preschooler

Child's Name Linsey Age 3 yrs. 9 mos.
Observer Beth Date 10·98

Check off the *areas of development* that apply:

- [x] Thinking, Reasoning & Problem-Solving
- [ ] Emotional and Social Competency
- [ ] Gross-Motor Development
- [ ] Fine-Motor Development
- [ ] Language and Communication
- [ ] Reading & Writing Development
- [ ] Creative Development

This photo, work sample and/or anecdote illustrates the following *developmental milestone(s):*

counts but not yet with 1:1 correspondence
uses measurement words and tools

Check off whatever applies to the context of this observation:

- [x] Child-initiated activity
- [ ] Teacher-initiated activity
- [x] New task for this child
- [ ] Familiar task for this child
- [x] Done independently
- [ ] Done with adult guidance
- [x] Done with peer(s)
- [x] Time spent (1-5 mins.)
- [ ] Time spent (5-15 mins.)
- [ ] Time spent (15+ mins.)

Anecdotal Note: Describe what you saw the child do and/or heard the child say.

Jordan and Noah had just built a tower. Jordan was measuring it with a ruler. Linsey got out the tape measure and pretended to measure. "Let's see how tall it is. One, two, three, nine..." Linsey talked to Jordan for a few minutes, then left.

Developmental Milestones Collection Form
Version #1 Preschooler

Child's Name Linsey   Age 3 yrs. 10 mos.
Observer Beth   Date 12-98

Check off the *areas of development* that apply:

- ☐ Thinking, Reasoning & Problem-Solving
- ☒ Emotional and Social Competency
- ☐ Gross-Motor Development
- ☐ Fine-Motor Development
- ☐ Language and Communication
- ☐ Reading & Writing Development
- ☐ Creative Development

This photo, work sample and/or anecdote illustrates the following *developmental milestone(s):*

plays alongside others but is beginning to play cooperatively as "being friends" becomes more important

Check off whatever applies to the context of this observation:

- ☒ Child-initiated activity
- ☐ Teacher-initiated activity
- ☐ New task for this child
- ☒ Familiar task for this child
- ☐ Done independently
- ☐ Done with adult guidance
- ☒ Done with peer(s)
- ☒ Time spent (1-5 mins.)
- ☐ Time spent (5-15 mins.)
- ☐ Time spent (15+ mins.)

Anecdotal Note: Describe what you saw the child do and/or heard the child say.

Several of the children used the pegboards to make birthday cakes. They then had a celebration with Brandon's Mom.

Developmental Milestones Collection Form
Version #1 Preschooler

Child's Name Linsey Age 3yrs. 9 mos.
Observer Beth Date 11-98

Check off the *areas of development* that apply:

- ❑ Thinking, Reasoning & Problem-Solving
- ❑ Emotional and Social Competency
- ☒ Gross-Motor Development
- ❑ Fine-Motor Development
- ❑ Language and Communication
- ❑ Reading & Writing Development
- ❑ Creative Development

This photo, work sample and/or anecdote illustrates the following *developmental milestone(s):*

balances with emerging skill; is developing coordination in a variety of situations

Check off whatever applies to the context of this observation:

- ☒ Child-initiated activity
- ❑ Teacher-initiated activity
- ❑ New task for this child
- ☒ Familiar task for this child
- ❑ Done independently
- ❑ Done with adult guidance
- ☒ Done with peer(s)
- ❑ Time spent (1-5 mins.)
- ☒ Time spent (5-15 mins.)
- ❑ Time spent (15+ mins.)

Anecdotal Note: Describe what you saw the child do and/or heard the child say.

In our outdoor play yard, Linsey is becoming more active and trying new things that involve climbing and balancing. She now gets to the top of the climber quickly with no adult help.

Developmental Milestones Collection Form
Version #1 Preschooler

Child's Name Linsey Age 3 yrs. 9 mos.
Observer Beth Date 11-98

Check off the *areas of development* that apply:

- ❑ Thinking, Reasoning & Problem-Solving
- ❑ Emotional and Social Competency
- ❑ Gross-Motor Development
- ☒ Fine-Motor Development
- ❑ Language and Communication
- ❑ Reading & Writing Development
- ❑ Creative Development

This photo, work sample and/or anecdote illustrates the following *developmental milestone(s):*

uses small puzzle pieces (12 piece puzzle)

Check off whatever applies to the context of this observation:

- ☒ Child-initiated activity
- ❑ Teacher-initiated activity
- ❑ New task for this child
- ☒ Familiar task for this child
- ☒ Done independently
- ❑ Done with adult guidance
- ❑ Done with peer(s)
- ❑ Time spent (1-5 mins.)
- ☒ Time spent (5-15 mins.)
- ❑ Time spent (15+ mins.)

Anecdotal Note: Describe what you saw the child do and/or heard the child say.

Linsey was singing as she went to the puzzle shelf. She worked on this puzzle for more than 5 mins., trying to fit the pieces and singing. She did not ask for help. When she completed the puzzle, she left the table. I asked her to put the puzzle back on the shelf and she quickly complied and went off to play elsewhere.

(see photo attached)

Focused Portfolios™ Photo

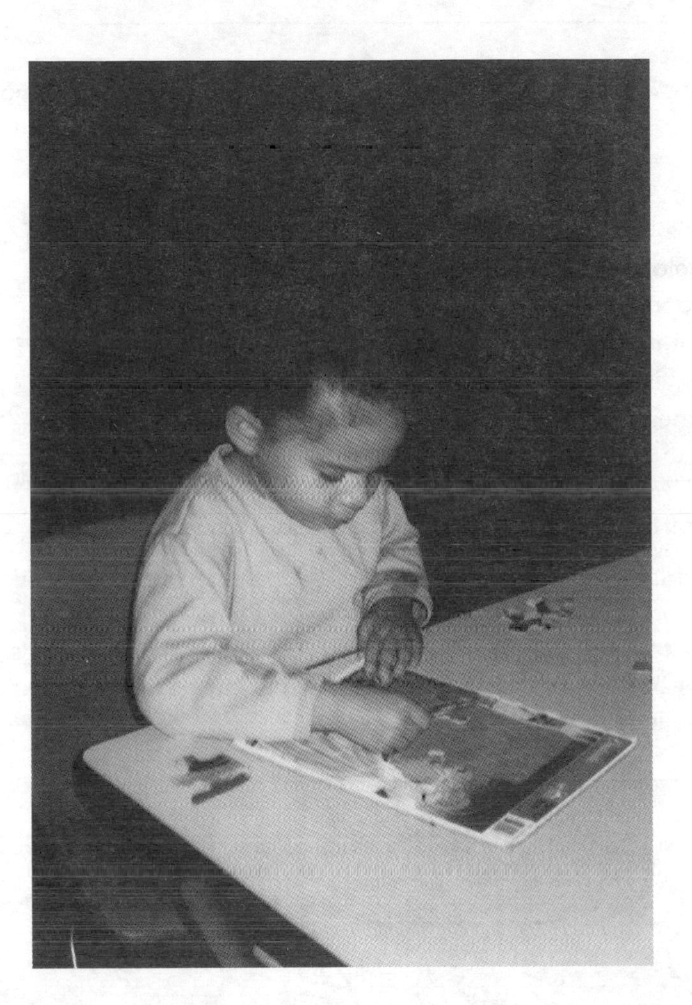

Developmental Milestones Collection Form
Version #1 Preschooler

Child's Name Linsey Age 3yrs. 10mos.
Observer Beth Date 12-14-99

Check off the *areas of development* that apply:

- ❑ Thinking, Reasoning & Problem-Solving
- ❑ Emotional and Social Competency
- ❑ Gross-Motor Development
- ❑ Fine-Motor Development
- ☒ Language and Communication
- ❑ Reading & Writing Development
- ❑ Creative Development

This photo, work sample and/or anecdote illustrates the following *developmental milestone(s)*:

can retell a basic story sequence
learns words to simple songs and stories

Check off whatever applies to the context of this observation:

- ❑ Child-initiated activity
- ☒ Teacher-initiated activity
- ❑ New task for this child
- ❑ Familiar task for this child
- ❑ Done independently
- ❑ Done with adult guidance
- ☒ Done with peer(s)
- ❑ Time spent (1-5 mins.)
- ☒ Time spent (5-15 mins.)
- ❑ Time spent (15+ mins.)

Anecdotal Note: Describe what you saw the child do and/or heard the child say.

Today, we acted out the story, "The Three Little Pigs." Linsey asked to be the Big Bad Wolf. She loudly sang, "Mud, Glorious Mud," and remembered all the lines of the wolf with each pig. She asked to do it a second and third time.

Developmental Milestones Collection Form
Version #1 Preschooler

Child's Name: Linsey   Age: 3 yrs. 8 mos.

Observer: Beth   Date: 11-7-98

Check off the *areas of development* that apply:

- ☐ Thinking, Reasoning & Problem-Solving
- ☐ Emotional and Social Competency
- ☐ Gross-Motor Development
- ☐ Fine-Motor Development
- ☐ Language and Communication
- ☒ Reading & Writing Development
- ☐ Creative Development

This photo, work sample and/or anecdote illustrates the following *developmental milestone(s):*

plays at reading and writing

Check off whatever applies to the context of this observation:

- ☒ Child-initiated activity
- ☐ Teacher-initiated activity
- ☐ New task for this child
- ☐ Familiar task for this child
- ☒ Done independently
- ☐ Done with adult guidance
- ☐ Done with peer(s)
- ☐ Time spent (1-5 mins.)
- ☒ Time spent (5-15 mins.)
- ☐ Time spent (15+ mins.)

Anecdotal Note: Describe what you saw the child do and/or heard the child say.

Linsey talks aloud as she writes a letter in the housekeeping area. "Dear Grandma, I am coming to visit you." She occasionally follows along with her finger underneath what she has written, moving from left to right and top to bottom. She shows much interest in reading and writing.

Developmental Milestones Collection Form
Version #1 Preschooler

Child's Name Linsey Age 3 yrs. 8 mos.
Observer Beth Date 10-21-98

Check off the *areas of development* that apply:

- ❑ Thinking, Reasoning & Problem-Solving
- ❑ Emotional and Social Competency
- ❑ Gross-Motor Development
- ❑ Fine-Motor Development
- ❑ Language and Communication
- ❑ Reading & Writing Development
- ☒ Creative Development

This photo, work sample and/or anecdote illustrates the following *developmental milestone(s):*

explores a variety of expressive media

Check off whatever applies to the context of this observation:

- ❑ Child-initiated activity
- ☒ Teacher-initiated activity
- ❑ New task for this child
- ☒ Familiar task for this child
- ☒ Done independently
- ❑ Done with adult guidance
- ❑ Done with peer(s)
- ☒ Time spent (1-5 mins.)
- ❑ Time spent (5-15 mins.)
- ❑ Time spent (15+ mins.)

Anecdotal Note: Describe what you saw the child do and/or heard the child say.

We had just read a book, "Dem Bones," and talked about our bones and body parts. Linsey began to paint a skeleton - then when her neighbor left, she took his brush. She continued to paint with 2 brushes at once and said, "My Mom and Dad are dancing."

Focused Portfolios™ Reflection and Planning Form

Child's Name Linsey Age 4 Teacher Beth Date 12/98

Teacher Reflection

Refer to all *areas of development* and to the items in the portfolio

Summarize information from Favorites, Friends, and Family:

Linsey has many interests in our classroom – blocks, animals, dress-up, puzzles and art. She often plays alone or with Brandon. Thank you for helping so regularly in the classroom.

List milestones accomplished:

- explores immediate environment
- begins to generate ideas
- uses measurement tools/words
- over time, shows comfort with new people
- manages routines such as clean-up
- uses puzzles (12 pieces)
- retells basic story sequence
- plays at reading & writing
- explores variety of expressive media

Describe progress that has been observed:

Linsey's block play and make-believe play continue to grow in complexity and imagination. She's become far more of a risk-taker outside climbing.

List the milestones that this child is working on (these are the goals for the next collection):

- counts objects using 1:1 correspondence
- verbalizes cause & effect when solving problems
- still plays alongside others but is beginning to play cooperatively
- works hard to use language to express feelings, negotiate
- is curious about letters and words

Family and Teacher Planning

Discuss plans to support further development. Write ideas for classroom activities, family involvement, and teacher support. Add any general comments.

Teacher: We are patiently allowing Linsey to find her own way of communicating in the classroom. She is not a big "talker" and we want to accept her quiet way of joining activities. She's more verbal in dramatic play, acting out stories. So, we'll provide her more of that.

Will invite Linsey to count objects in everyday activities like setting the table for snack. With her curiosity about reading and writing, her interest and recognition of letters will grow. We'll join her at the writing center and library.

Family member(s):

There's such a difference in how much Linsey talks at home and school. There's hardly a moment at home when she's not talking! I support your goals for Linsey to help her talk and join in more. I think preschool helps her a lot. We'll count at home. We read books every day and she loves to go to the library.

Thanks for helping me and Linsey.

Marsha

chapter 4

Favorites Collection Form
Child's Name Brandon
Observer Beth
Date October 1998

> The Documentation Process

Now that you have a sense of the four categories for collecting in this portfolio process, you are ready to learn more about the steps involved in documentation. The documentation process includes developing observation skills, planning for documentation, writing factual observation notes, and taking good photographs. Some of the steps are the same no matter what the purpose of the documentation. And some of the steps are different depending on whether you are collecting evidence of children's favorites, friends, family, or developmental milestones.

> Skillful Observation

Observing children carefully and writing accurate and informative anecdotes are essential aspects of purposeful portfolio collection. These are skills that all teachers, whether new to the classroom or seasoned professionals, can continue to improve with practice.

Developing skillful observation is like developing strong muscles. Working the muscle regularly gives you added strength, stamina, and flexibility. Like an athlete preparing for a competitive event, teachers must continually work at flexing their "observation muscles" and sharpening their observation skills.

In your classroom, you are probably observing children much of the time. You know the importance of providing children with a sense of safety and control by always being able to see the children throughout the room. With a teacher's super-sensitive hearing, the phrase "eyes in the back of the head" really rings true. Teachers sense where children are and whether things are running smoothly or an adult needs to intervene.

However, you may not be writing down what you have seen the children do. For many teachers, observation "just happens"—it is not planned or documented.

It's important to recognize and value the amount of observation you already do. At the same time, you can move toward regular recording of children's interests, playmates, family events, and developmental accomplishments. By systematically observing and documenting these areas, you will know the children better. And you will raise your accountability by having concrete information to share with families.

> Two Ways to Approach Documentation

There are two ways to approach documentation of your everyday activities with the children:

1. Planning ahead
2. Reflecting back

Planning ahead involves making some decisions before you observe and take notes. It may mean focusing observation on particular children or activities, or identifying the specific areas of the portfolio for which you are observing. You plan to watch children with a particular focus, such as one or more of the following:

- a child's preferred activities or playmates
- a specific area of development
- a child's use of particular materials
- an individual goal (like an Individual Education Plan (IEP) goal or learning objective)

Reflecting back happens after the observation is done. You may think about what you saw, look through your anecdotes, review your photos and work samples, or glance through the Developmental Milestones Charts to determine what documentation you want to record for the portfolio. Having stepped away from the classroom, you think about the meaning of what you already observed. Sometimes what you've learned about the children becomes clear after the fact.

Each of these approaches has advantages and disadvantages depending on individual teaching and organizational styles. Planning ahead helps make sure that no child or area of development is missed. Reflecting back enables you to put more "pieces of the puzzle" together at a later time. Most teachers choose to do some of each, trying to achieve balance between them.

Planning Ahead for Favorites, Friends, Family, and Developmental Milestones

When you are planning ahead, you focus your observations of children specifically on examples of their frequent choices for the Favorites form, or their consistent playmates for the Friends form, or you try to find examples of one particular area of development. You may write in your plans that you will be looking at how infants and toddlers show their excitement when their family members arrive at pickup time. Or you may look for examples of preschoolers' budding social skills as they ask a friend to play with them. You will watch to see how infants and toddlers express feelings or demonstrate self-awareness. Or you may look for examples of preschoolers' emotional and social competency.

Planning ahead may mean providing specific materials with the idea of collecting a work sample. Let's say you want to learn more about your toddlers' emerging fine-motor skills. You put out big, fat crayons or water-based markers and paper, and encourage children to draw and write on the paper.

In this way, you are planning to document the specific fine-motor milestones about how toddlers scribble with markers or crayon and imitate a horizontal crayon stroke. When you collect a sample of scribbling from a toddler, you still fill out the collection form and staple it directly to the child's work. In this case, there's no waiting for photography development. You may even have a quote from the child as he said, "Me did it! My picture!" All of this can be noted on the collection form.

If you decide to focus on preschoolers' creative development, you make sure that the art area in your classroom is well stocked with paper, scissors, glue, and paints. Then you encourage children to go over to that area and express their creativity in whatever way they like. You may choose to sit at the art table with the children or stand near the art easels. At either place, as children use the materials, you carefully observe and record what you see directly onto the collection forms. You can also note what you hear the children say about their creations.

While observing, note the amount of control individual children have over the tools they are using, and whether they choose to name objects in their creation, or talk about the colors and shapes involved in the design. These informative details add richness to descriptions. When you collect the painting, drawing, or collage from the child, complete the collection form and staple it directly to the child's work.

You may find you get a better, more accurate sample of children's creativity if you provide them with repeated opportunities to explore the materials in the art area. You want your sample to be truly reflective of what each child can do.

If you teach young children with identified special needs, the Individual Family Service Plan (IFSP) or IEP goals may help you plan for documentation. You may focus on how a child with physical disabilities uses adaptive equipment to stand at the water table or lie down to read a book. As you observe this child in action, you pay particular attention to his actions that are tied to these important goals, and note them on the appropriate collection form.

Making Sure to Collect Documentation on All the Children

Another way to plan ahead is to focus observations on specific children. Every teacher is busy. There are many little voices to listen to, hands to guide, strong feelings to help control, and classroom duties to perform. Sometimes children who do not demand a lot of attention, or who seem able to manage pretty well, may not be observed in the natural flow of daily activities. It's as if they almost "disappear" because they fit in so well. You may need to plan ahead to observe those children more closely so you can learn more about their growth and development, and celebrate their accomplishments.

Some teachers identify certain children each day that they will observe. By doing so they make sure that, over time, no one is missed. You may choose to include in your written plans, or identify with your teaching colleagues, the names of those children who will be observed each day. In chapter 5, we will introduce several tips and tools that will help you keep track of which children have been observed and how often.

Reflecting Back

When you are reflecting back, you do not plan for documentation. Moreover, some teachers report that while they are in the middle of the action with children, they are not focused on specific areas to observe. Instead, they find that those areas become more evident to them when they think back and reflect away from the action. Many times the connection is made after the fact.

These teachers schedule reflection time at the end of each day (perhaps ten minutes). They review a class list and make notes about interactions and events that occurred during the day with specific children. As they look back over the day, they think about children's choices, interests, and playmates, and refer to the Developmental Milestones Charts. Then they write anecdotes directly on the appropriate collection forms.

For example, during the morning a teacher had witnessed an infant feeding himself.

Later, on her break, she checked the Developmental Milestones Charts and realized that this event demonstrated the child's growing competence in the area of Acts with Purpose and Uses Tools. On a collection form, she checked off the appropriate area of development, wrote the milestone in the space, and added details about the child's use of a cup and spoon.

Another opportunity for reflecting back occurs when teachers pick up the prints after film has been developed (or downloaded into the computer when using a digital camera). Many teachers find that as they review the photos they've taken of the children in action, they remember specifics about those situations and can write detailed anecdotes. Reviewing photos with the Developmental Milestones Charts nearby helps teachers connect the activity observed to developmental information.

Reflecting back is a viable approach to documentation, but a word of caution is necessary: When you rely on reflecting back as the only time to record observations, you sharply increase the possibility of writing subjective anecdotes. Again, we urge you to strive for balance in the use of planning ahead and reflecting back.

> Writing the All-Important Anecdote

The anecdote is important because it's how you capture what a child did or said, what you saw and heard. Observing without documenting your observation does not provide you with a written, factual record of children's achievements. Objective anecdotes give the portfolio its authenticity—and increase your reliability and accountability. You are not relying solely on your memory or reconstructing what you think happened. Instead, you are carefully recording your observations.

On the following pages, you will find examples of photos with and without anecdotes. First, review the examples of photos without anecdotes. Consider:

- What do these photos tell you about the learners?
- What questions come to mind as you look at these items?
- What information is missing by just having the item and not an accompanying description?

Then review the same photos on collection forms with anecdotes.

- What does this photo and the accompanying anecdote tell you about this learner?
- Do the same questions come to mind as they did when there were no descriptions?
- Have some of your previous questions been answered?

The photos and work samples alone do not provide sufficient documentation to show and explain progress. But when they are accompanied by a teacher's anecdote—a written note describing what was happening with the child at the time the photo was taken or the work sample was produced—the documentation is enhanced. The anecdote tells a story of the process the child was engaged in—what you, the teacher, observed the child doing, or heard the child saying, or helped the child to achieve. The description adds depth, context, and perspective.

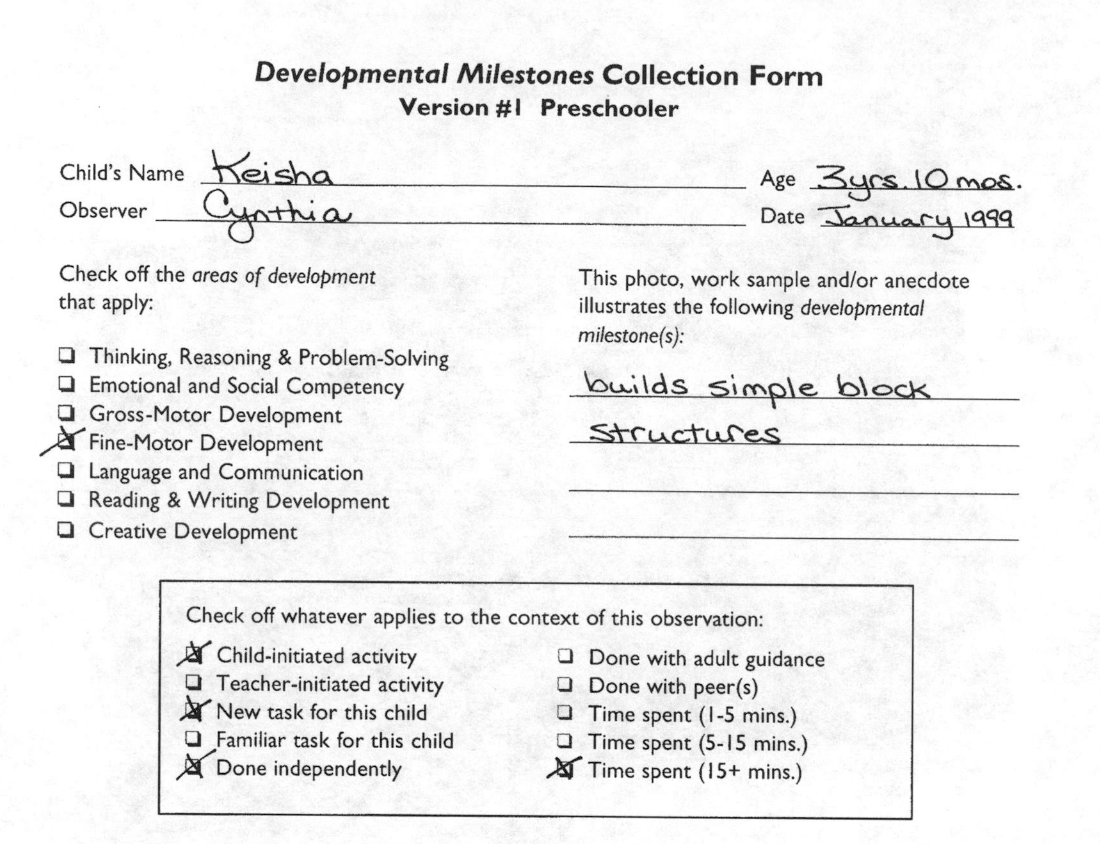

Developmental Milestones Collection Form
Version #1 Preschooler

Child's Name Keisha Age 3yrs. 10 mos.
Observer Cynthia Date January 1999

Check off the *areas of development* that apply:

- [ ] Thinking, Reasoning & Problem-Solving
- [ ] Emotional and Social Competency
- [ ] Gross-Motor Development
- [x] Fine-Motor Development
- [ ] Language and Communication
- [ ] Reading & Writing Development
- [ ] Creative Development

This photo, work sample and/or anecdote illustrates the following *developmental milestone(s):*

builds simple block structures

Check off whatever applies to the context of this observation:

- [x] Child-initiated activity
- [ ] Teacher-initiated activity
- [x] New task for this child
- [ ] Familiar task for this child
- [x] Done independently
- [ ] Done with adult guidance
- [ ] Done with peer(s)
- [ ] Time spent (1-5 mins.)
- [ ] Time spent (5-15 mins.)
- [x] Time spent (15+ mins.)

Anecdotal Note: Describe what you saw the child do and/or heard the child say.

Keisha went to the Manipulative Toy Area today toward the 2nd part of Choice Time. She found the Duplos on the Table where other children had left them. No one else was working in the area at the time. She put the bin of Duplos on the floor and began to erect this construction (see photo) on the base. She worked quietly, sometimes whispering to herself until she was done. Then, she came over to me, took my hand and, smiling, said, "Teacher, come see what I made." I later realized this was the 1st time I had observed Keisha using Duplos in the classroom.

(see photo attached)

Focused Portfolios™ Photo

Developmental Milestones Collection Form
Version #1 Infant/Toddler

Child's Name Emily Age 20 months
Observer Stephen Date July 7, 1998

Check off the *areas of development* that apply:

- ❑ Shows interest in others
- ❑ Demonstrates self-awareness
- ❑ Accomplishes gross-motor milestones
- ❑ Accomplishes fine-motor milestones
- ❑ Communicates
- ❑ Acts with purpose and uses tools
- ❑ Expresses feelings

This photo, work sample and/or anecdote illustrates the following *developmental milestone(s):*

explores objects through touch

Check off whatever applies to the context of this observation:

- ❑ Child-initiated activity
- ☒ Teacher-initiated activity
- ☒ New task for this child
- ❑ Familiar task for this child
- ❑ Done independently
- ❑ Done with adult guidance
- ☒ Done with peer(s)
- ❑ Time spent (1-5 mins.)
- ☒ Time spent (5-15 mins.)
- ❑ Time spent (15+ mins.)

Anecdotal Note: Describe what you saw the child do and/or heard the child say.

Emily explored the smell and texture of the shaving cream. This is the first time she came to this activity, after watching others finger paint and paint with shaving cream for several weeks. She says, "Daddy" when asked who uses shaving cream in her house.

Factual vs. Interpretive Anecdotes

The documentation we are referring to here is not about writing your own thoughts and feelings about the child's actions. This type of anecdote is a factual record, not one based on your opinion. Accuracy is important. It usually takes a few observations to get enough factual information to come to an accurate interpretation of the child's behavior.

Interpretation does fit in the Focused Portfolios™ process. Evaluation of the child's growth and development is used in an ongoing way to plan and support further learning. For this reason, it is appropriate to interpret children's behavior. However, in recording observations on the collection forms, teachers should write only factual information about children's capabilities. In this way, you collect information about what the child is doing before you evaluate how the child is doing in order to avoid jumping to premature conclusions.

You will interpret and evaluate documentation after you have been collecting portfolio pieces for about three months. Your evaluation will be written on a special report called the Reflection and Planning Form. More about writing this evaluation and conferencing with families is included in chapter 8.

Here are some examples of anecdotal notes that are subjective. Then, we give examples of the same anecdotes rewritten to be factual and descriptive.

Subjective "Missy loves to play with the activity board. When she bats at a button and makes a noise or moves the spinning ball, she smiles and giggles, kicking her legs and moving her arms rapidly. She is such a happy baby!"

Factual and Descriptive "When we place Missy in front of the activity board, she smiles and giggles. She kicks her legs and moves her arms rapidly whenever she hits one of the buttons and it makes a noise or moves the spinning ball. She does not cry while engaged with the activity board."

Subjective "Todd really enjoys playdough. He likes to pound it and pull it and is beginning to roll it so he can use thinner pieces. It seems like this is his favorite thing to do at school."

Factual and Descriptive "Todd chooses to play with playdough almost daily. He pounds it and pulls it and is beginning to roll it into thin strips. He said, 'Playdough is my favorite thing at school.'"

In writing a factual anecdote, there are words and phrases that are more interpretive and ones that are more objective. Here's a table of suggestions. Can you think of others?

Words & Phrases to Avoid	Words & Phrases to Use
• The child loves . . .	• He often chooses . . .
• The child likes . . .	• I saw him . . .
• He enjoys . . .	• I heard her say . . .
• She spends a long time at . . .	• He spends five minutes doing . . .
• It seems like . . .	• She said . . .
• It appears . . .	• Almost every day he . . .
• I thought . . .	• Once or twice a month, she . . .
• I felt . . .	• Each time, he . . .
• I wonder . . .	• She consistently . . .
• He does . . . very well . . .	• We observed a pattern of . . .
• She is bad at . . .	
• This is difficult for . . .	

Every teacher has stories of misinterpreting a child's behavior or developmental skills. For example, a new child starts in your program. This child flits around the classroom, moving quickly from one activity to another, staying a minimum of a minute or two at each activity. As you observe this behavior, your initial interpretation might be that this child has an extremely short attention span and difficulty focusing or becoming engaged in meaningful activities. However, after a short time, this child's behavior has changed dramatically. He now settles into favorite activities easily and stays for long periods of time. Your initial interpretation was wrong. Over time, you witnessed more instances of what this child was able to do and could now interpret your documentation differently: This child was excited to be at your program and was exploring all the new possibilities offered. Once the initial excitement wore off, he demonstrated a long attention span and engaged in a variety of activities.

It's important that you write down only factual descriptions of what you see the child doing or hear the child saying. As you do so, you may be asking yourself some interpretive questions. But those questions are a form of reflection on your part. You are thinking about this child—"Who is she? What does she like? How does she show her personality, strengths, and weaknesses? I wonder why she does such-and-such?" Most teachers do not write down these questions—although there is nothing the matter with doing so. Instead, they pause and think about each of their children. If you should wish to write down your reflection questions, do not include them as part of your anecdote. Keep the anecdote as your factual record of the child's actions. You can keep a separate journal for your thoughts and questions.

As you continue to observe the child, you are collecting information either to support your initial interpretations and questions or to change them. You are also continually gathering information that will affect your curricular planning. For example, when you observe and document that a four-year-old counts up to four items consistently with one-to-one correspondence, you make a judgment that this child can now be challenged to move on to other counting activities beyond four objects. What you write down in your observations is exactly what the child did or said—the factual, detailed description of the counting activity. What you may reflect upon in your own thinking is "Wow, Shelley's counting up to four. Time to take out a board game with dice."

Sometimes, your factual observation notes aren't as clear-cut as the counting example. Consider this next situation. An infant is crabby over a period of days. You check carefully for physical problems. You ask yourself, "What's going on with this child?" Perhaps changes in caregivers at school or disruption of routines at home need to be explored as possible causes for fussiness. Close observation over time, combined with information from the family, may lead all of you to realize the child is teething. You can then act to soothe those sore gums by providing ice-cold teethers for relief.

On the collection forms for Favorites, Friends, Family, and Developmental Milestones, we have included a space for a detailed description of your observation. The question to ask yourself is always "What does this photo or this work sample tell me about this learner?" Your description can be one way to answer that question. By telling more about how the child went about the activity, you are capturing on paper, for yourself and others, what this child is learning to do.

The Stand-Alone Anecdote

There are times when a description by itself can be sufficient documentation. Such an anecdote can be written right on the collection form in the space provided.

The stand-alone anecdote should be detailed enough to create a picture in the reader's mind. If clearly written, the description will carefully set the stage, tell the context in which the observation took place, and explain exactly what the child said or did. Such extensive detail may not be necessary when an anecdote accompanies a photo or work sample, because the photo or sample will also communicate to the family or another teacher what the child was doing or producing. However, to stand alone, a description should indeed be detailed so that it reflects accurately what was observed.

On the next page is an example of a stand-alone anecdote that is not detailed enough.

- What does this anecdote tell you about this learner?
- What questions come to mind as you look at it?
- What information is missing?

On page 101 is an example of a more detailed stand-alone anecdote. After reading this second description:

- Do you know more about his growth and development?
- Have some of your previous questions been answered?
- Do you still need more information than the teacher has provided in order to understand why the teacher included this description in this portfolio? If so, what details are missing?

Developmental Milestones Collection Form
Version #1 Preschooler

Child's Name Jamel Age 3.8 years
Observer John Date 4/24/96

Check off the *areas of development* that apply:

- ❑ Thinking, Reasoning & Problem-Solving
- ☒ Emotional and Social Competency
- ❑ Gross-Motor Development
- ❑ Fine-Motor Development
- ❑ Language and Communication
- ❑ Reading & Writing Development
- ❑ Creative Development

This photo, work sample and/or anecdote illustrates the following *developmental milestone(s):*

manages routines such as cleaning up after self; works hard to use language to express feelings, negotiate, & resolve disagreements, with adult help

Check off whatever applies to the context of this observation:

- ❑ Child-initiated activity
- ☒ Teacher-initiated activity
- ❑ New task for this child
- ☒ Familiar task for this child
- ❑ Done independently
- ❑ Done with adult guidance
- ☒ Done with peer(s)
- ☒ Time spent (1-5 mins.)
- ❑ Time spent (5-15 mins.)
- ❑ Time spent (15+ mins.)

Anecdotal Note: Describe what you saw the child do and/or heard the child say.

I asked Jamel to help Cinda, Ashley and Andre clean up the block area. He ran over and put away a couple of blocks. Andre yelled at him and Jamel Talked with Andre about helping.

Developmental Milestones Collection Form
Version #1 Preschooler

Child's Name Jamel Age 3.8 years
Observer John Date 4/24/96

Check off the *areas of development* that apply:

- ☐ Thinking, Reasoning & Problem-Solving
- ☒ Emotional and Social Competency
- ☐ Gross-Motor Development
- ☐ Fine-Motor Development
- ☐ Language and Communication
- ☐ Reading & Writing Development
- ☐ Creative Development

This photo, work sample and/or anecdote illustrates the following *developmental milestone(s):*

manages routines such as cleaning up after self; works hard to use language to express feelings, negotiate, & resolve disagreements, with adult help

Check off whatever applies to the context of this observation:

- ☐ Child-initiated activity
- ☒ Teacher-initiated activity
- ☐ New task for this child
- ☒ Familiar task for this child
- ☐ Done independently
- ☐ Done with adult guidance
- ☒ Done with peer(s)
- ☒ Time spent (1-5 mins.)
- ☐ Time spent (5-15 mins.)
- ☐ Time spent (15+ mins.)

Anecdotal Note: Describe what you saw the child do and/or heard the child say.

I asked Jamel to help Cinda, Ashley and Andre clean up the block area. He ran over & put away a couple of blocks. Andre yelled at him: "Wait Jamel, I'm the clean-up helper!" and pulled the blocks from Jamel's hand. Jamel put his hands on his hips & said, "Use your words, Andre. Don't take no blocks from me. I'm helping you. Then we can go outside faster," and turned to me & said, "Right, John?" I replied, "You've got that right!"

Andre stopped for a minute then said, "Okay," and the two of them finished the job with the girls.

Other Kinds of Anecdotes

The notes that accompany a photo or work sample do not always have to be simple sentences or descriptive phrases. There can be other ways to get information recorded quickly.

Language samples, or word lists, are an efficient way to document children's growing oral language and vocabulary. We have included a form, the Infant/Toddler Word List, for recording infants' and toddlers' growing vocabulary *(also see appendix A)*. Here are two copies of the Word List form: one is blank; the other is an example with a child's words recorded.

Infant/Toddler Word List

Child ______________________ Teacher(s) ______________________

Date:	Word Approximations, Words, and/or Word Combinations	Context (imitation, response to comment or question, self-initiated)

Anecdotal Comments:

Infant/Toddler Word List

Child Colin Teacher(s) Abbey

Date:	Word Approximations, Words and/or Word Combinations	Context (imitation, response to comment or question, self-initiated)
9/1/97	Doggie	points to and shouts out
	banana	
	juice	
	cheese	
	hi	
	Daddy	
	Mommy	
	Bye-bye	mostly when he's prompted
10/17/97	juice, please	asks for himself!
	night night	
	car	
	kitty cat	
	"moo"	in response to question, "what does the cow say?"
	ball	
	bear	
	bell	
	birthday	

Anecdotal Comments: Colin's language is growing every day. His speech is understandable much of the time and he tries hard to communicate what he sees or wants.

Documenting Preschoolers' Language

Documenting preschoolers' growing oral language and vocabulary can be done by using the Developmental Milestones Collection Form. In the area on the form reserved for the anecdotal note, write down a direct quote from the child. In this way, you'll be demonstrating how the child uses language in conversations with you or with other children. Here are some examples.

Heidi Wagreich, a speech pathologist in West Chicago, captures language samples from the preschoolers in her program. She includes an analysis of their growing skills in articulation (an IEP goal) as part of her documentation on the Developmental Milestones Collection Form, even though articulation is not a specific area on the Developmental Milestones Charts.

For her toddlers at the Indiana School for the Deaf, Connie Jones-McLean correlates her developmental milestones collection of growing communication skills directly to their IFSP goals of developing American Sign Language. One of her anecdotes described a child's demonstration of growing vocabulary on a field trip to the farm:

"Dylan patted the donkey. Mom signed 'donkey' to her. Later, Dylan signed 'donkey.'"

On the following pages you'll find two more examples of Developmental Milestones forms used to document children's growing language.

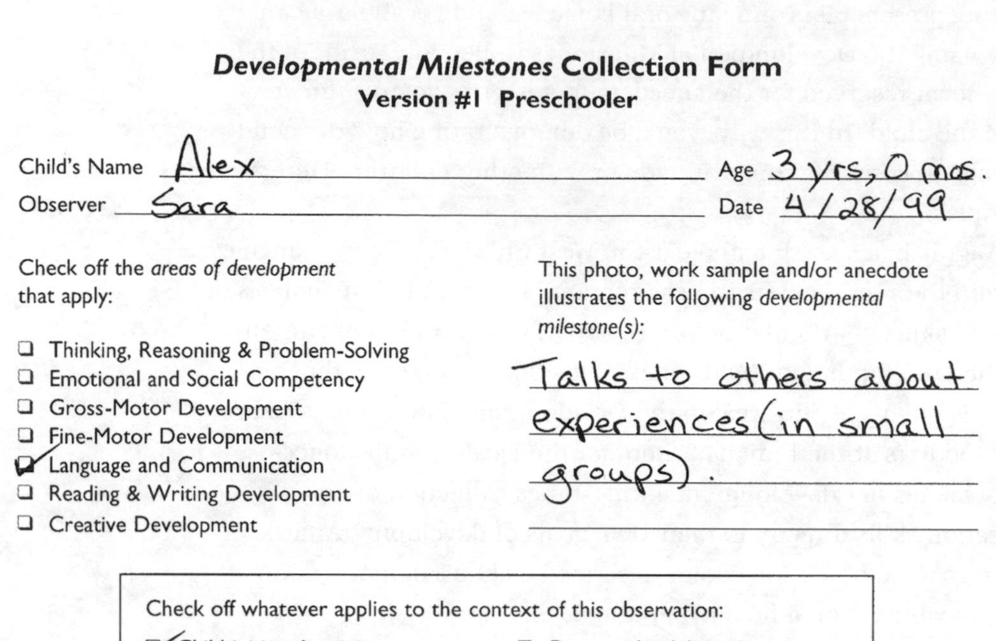

Developmental Milestones Collection Form
Version #1 Preschooler

Child's Name Alex Age 3 yrs, 0 mos.
Observer Sara Date 4/28/99

Check off the *areas of development* that apply:

- ❑ Thinking, Reasoning & Problem-Solving
- ❑ Emotional and Social Competency
- ❑ Gross-Motor Development
- ❑ Fine-Motor Development
- ☑ Language and Communication
- ❑ Reading & Writing Development
- ❑ Creative Development

This photo, work sample and/or anecdote illustrates the following *developmental milestone(s):*

Talks to others about experiences (in small groups).

Check off whatever applies to the context of this observation:

- ☑ Child-initiated activity
- ❑ Teacher-initiated activity
- ❑ New task for this child
- ❑ Familiar task for this child
- ❑ Done independently
- ❑ Done with adult guidance
- ❑ Done with peer(s)
- ❑ Time spent (1-5 mins.)
- ❑ Time spent (5-15 mins.)
- ❑ Time spent (15+ mins.)

Anecdotal Note: Describe what you saw the child do and/or heard the child say.

Cynthia commented to Alex, "I love your shoes!" I said, "Alex, you better watch out or Cynthia will want to wear your shoes!" Alex sat across from Cynthia, turned over Cynthia's foot and put her own foot against it. She said, "No, it's too big," and pointed to Cynthia's shoe. She had measured her foot against Cynthia's. She ended the conversation by saying, "These are my shoes, Cynthia."

Developmental Milestones Collection Form
Version #1 Preschooler

Child's Name Kyle Age 4
Observer Linda Date 9/14/97

Check off the *areas of development* that apply:

- ❑ Thinking, Reasoning & Problem-Solving
- ❑ Emotional and Social Competency
- ❑ Gross-Motor Development
- ❑ Fine-Motor Development
- ☑ Language and Communication
- ❑ Reading & Writing Development
- ❑ Creative Development

This photo, work sample and/or anecdote illustrates the following *developmental milestone(s):*

Talks to others about experiences (in small groups).

Check off whatever applies to the context of this observation:

- ❑ Child-initiated activity
- ☑ Teacher-initiated activity
- ❑ New task for this child
- ❑ Familiar task for this child
- ❑ Done independently
- ❑ Done with adult guidance
- ❑ Done with peer(s)
- ❑ Time spent (1-5 mins.)
- ❑ Time spent (5-15 mins.)
- ❑ Time spent (15+ mins.)

Anecdotal Note: Describe what you saw the child do and/or heard the child say.

During Circle Time, in response to my questions, "What's your name and who's in your family?" Kyle replied, "I'm Kyle . . . My mom, Deanna, my dad, Richard, Sammi, my sister and Dayton." When I asked, "Where do you live?" he said, "I live a long ways from school."

> Taking Good Photos of Infants, Toddlers and Preschoolers

For portfolio documentation, the best photos are those of children actively engaged in an activity. As you read through these next pages, we will refer you to specific photos to illustrate key points.

As a general rule, do not ask children to pose. Asking a child to stop what he or she is doing and smile for the camera does not provide a photo that tells you something about what the child is doing. Instead, use the camera to capture a moment that clearly shows the child's investment and interest in the task at hand.

Look at the photos below of Malik in his walker and Nicholas posing with his construction. It is clear that the camera did not capture active engagement. What can you figure out about their development from these photos?

In the photos below of Josh reading to Kennie and of Alexandra pretending to pour cereal at the table, the teachers have successfully captured active engagement. As a result, what can you figure out about the development of these children?

Have a plan for your photos. Before you take a picture, ask yourself, "What does this tell me about how this child is growing and learning?" Do not take the picture if you are unsure of the answer.

Darla Peterson, director at King's Kids in Pekin, Illinois, thought ahead about the potential photography problems her teachers might encounter and had them practice with a twelve-shot roll of film. They were able to address technical problems that arose, such as backlighting, as well as documentation problems such as choosing incidents that really did not lend themselves to showing children engaged in meaningful activity.

Plan for the categories that you are trying to document. Is this an example of a favorite, a friend, or a representation of the child's family? Is it showing you something about the child's progress toward a developmental milestone? If not, you may wish to save your film for another opportunity.

Here are three photos to illustrate documenting favorites, developmental milestones, and family (Tyrell, Emily B., and Emily A.). As you look through these, also consider the element of active engagement.

Favorites Collection Form

Child's Name Tyrell Date 4/12/99

Observer Sharon

After observing the child on multiple occasions, describe a favorite activity that the child does often. Add details that you've noticed about the child's interests and choices. Add a photo if you can.

Description: When we place Tyrell in front of the mirror, he waves his hands excitedly and squeals loudly. Sometimes he stares straight ahead for several minutes, and then laughs and kicks his feet. His arm movements sometimes result in his hitting the mirror with a toy. When this occurs, he stops for a moment, then starts waving his arms again. If he is somewhere else in the room and is able to see the mirror, he looks over and makes sounds. We wonder if this is his way of "asking" to be put near the mirror.

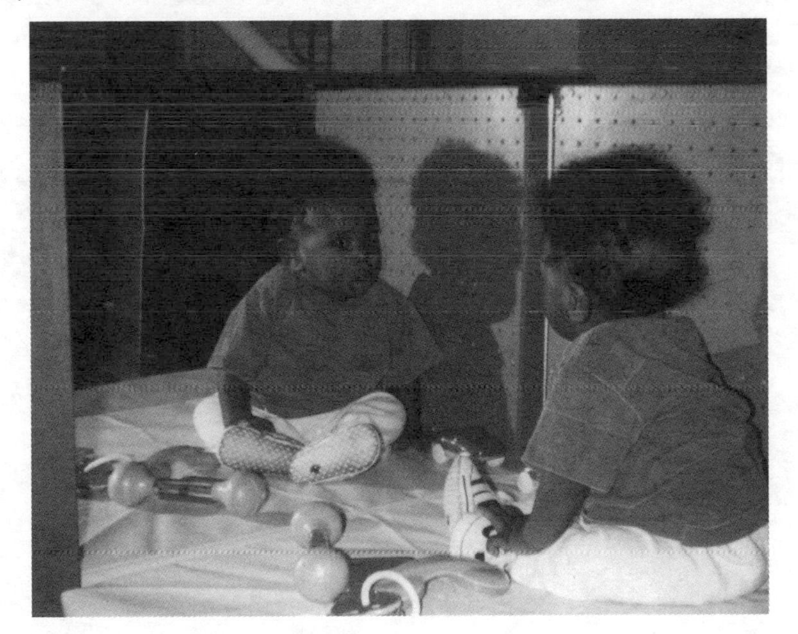

Developmental Milestones Collection Form
Version #1 Infant/Toddler

Child's Name EMILY B. Age 21 MONTHS
Observer MELISSA Date 8/19/98

Check off the *areas of development* that apply:

- ❑ Shows interest in others
- ❑ Demonstrates self-awareness
- ☒ Accomplishes gross-motor milestones
- ❑ Accomplishes fine-motor milestones
- ❑ Communicates
- ❑ Acts with purpose and uses tools
- ❑ Expresses feelings

This photo, work sample and/or anecdote illustrates the following *developmental milestone(s):*

CAUTIOUSLY WALKS UP & DOWN STAIRS;
MOVES AROUND OBJECTS

Check off whatever applies to the context of this observation:

- ☒ Child-initiated activity
- ❑ Teacher-initiated activity
- ❑ New task for this child
- ☒ Familiar task for this child
- ❑ Done independently
- ❑ Done with adult guidance
- ❑ Done with peer(s)
- ❑ Time spent (1-5 mins.)
- ☒ Time spent (5-15 mins.)
- ❑ Time spent (15+ mins.)

Anecdotal Note: Describe what you saw the child do and/or heard the child say.

EMILY WALKED UP AND DOWN THE PLAYGROUND STEPS, USING ALTERNATING FEET. SHE SPENT 7 MINUTES REPEATEDLY GOING UP AND DOWN.

Focused Portfolios™ Photo

Family Collection Form

Child's Name Emily A. Date December 14, 1998

Observer Beth

Families often have stories to share about their child's accomplishments at home. They also have special moments with their child in your classroom. Use this form to document a story that the child's family has shared with you, or take a photo of a special moment between the child and the people who are important in his or her life.

Description:

when Emily's mom and baby brother came to visit our classroom, she and Amanda took turns "reading" to the baby. Emily said to Amanda: "Read him this (handing her Brown Bear, Brown Bear). It's his favorite." While Amanda turned the pages, Emily talked to her brother in a high-pitched voice, repeating the words of the book and enunciating clearly.

Dealing with "Take My Picture, Teacher"

Introducing a camera into your room can sometimes have unanticipated results. Some children may stop what they are doing in order to "be in a picture." It may take a little time to get beyond this type of reaction. One teacher offered this helpful tip: "I tell the children that my camera likes to see them working and playing." She reported that in a very short time, children realized that they were more likely to have their picture taken if they were engaged in activities rather than posing for the camera.

Deanna Walker, an infant/toddler teacher at Springer Early Education Care Center in New Mexico, used her digital camera to take photos of various children's ongoing accomplishments. However, when she downloaded the photos, she found that C.J., an eighteen-month-old, appeared in several of the pictures. She realized that C.J. was very aware of when she was photographing other children and hurried across the room to be included in the pictures. Deanna recognized that this demonstrated C.J.'s growing sense of self and ability to act with purpose and intent, and noted that on a Developmental Milestones Collection Form for C.J.

Occasionally, a posed photo is okay. A group of children who are very proud of a block structure may wish to pose next to it. You then are documenting the result of their hard work and cooperative effort. The posing does not diminish that. Just be sure to include information about their process in the anecdote you write to accompany the posed photo.

Documenting special friends or a favorite activity may still be effective with the child smiling at the camera. You can make decisions about what is best but will want to keep in mind this question: "What does this tell me about how this child is growing and learning?"

Now look at the following photos of Kyle and Matthew. They do show children who have stopped and looked at the camera. Read the documentation that accompanies each photo. Decide for yourself: Are these poses still informative when you put them together with the teacher's observation notes?

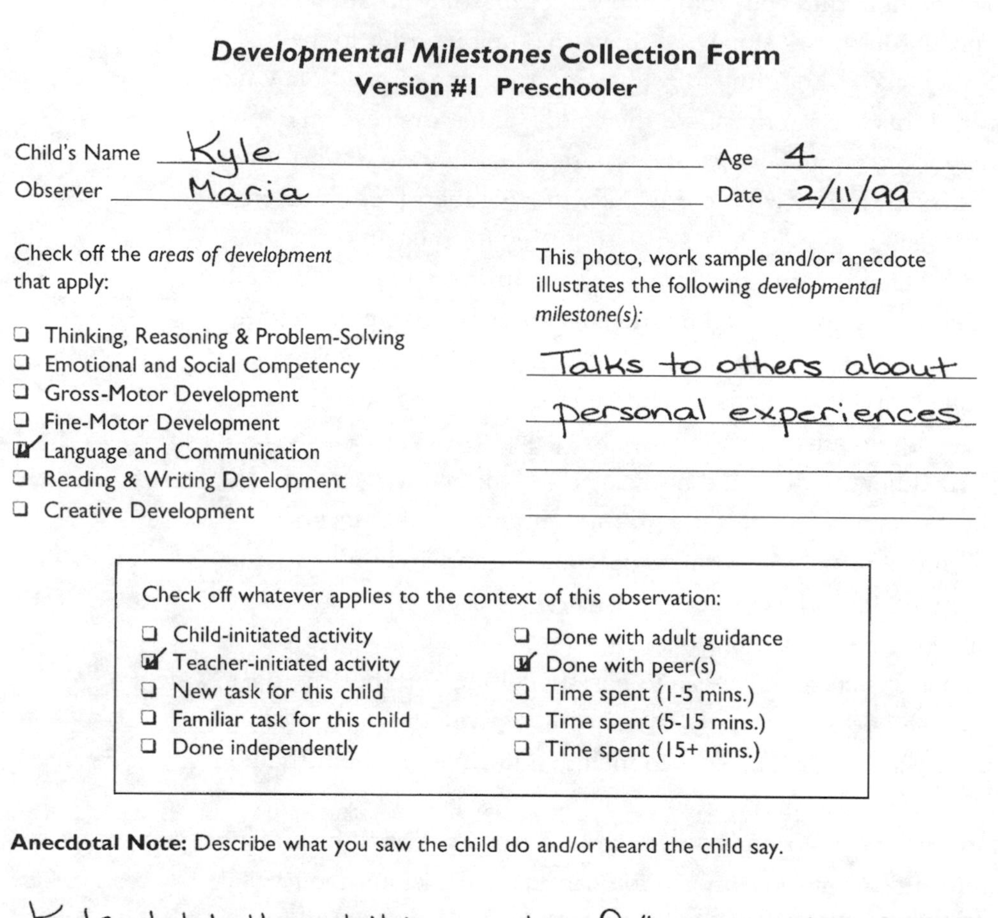

Developmental Milestones Collection Form
Version #1 Preschooler

Child's Name Kyle Age 4
Observer Maria Date 2/11/99

Check off the *areas of development* that apply:

- ☐ Thinking, Reasoning & Problem-Solving
- ☐ Emotional and Social Competency
- ☐ Gross-Motor Development
- ☐ Fine-Motor Development
- ☑ Language and Communication
- ☐ Reading & Writing Development
- ☐ Creative Development

This photo, work sample and/or anecdote illustrates the following *developmental milestone(s):*

Talks to others about personal experiences

Check off whatever applies to the context of this observation:

- ☐ Child-initiated activity
- ☑ Teacher-initiated activity
- ☐ New task for this child
- ☐ Familiar task for this child
- ☐ Done independently
- ☐ Done with adult guidance
- ☑ Done with peer(s)
- ☐ Time spent (1-5 mins.)
- ☐ Time spent (5-15 mins.)
- ☐ Time spent (15+ mins.)

Anecdotal Note: Describe what you saw the child do and/or heard the child say.

Kyle told the children the following about his mailbox:

Kyle: "My mom used a shoe box and she used construction paper. I did this. I decorated it."

Maria: "How did you decorate it?"

Kyle: "With markers. Mom did the tree and the sun. I wrote my name. I did the 'k'. See this lid? You open it like this."

(see attached photo)

Focused Portfolios™ Photo

Developmental Milestones Collection Form
Version #1 Infant/Toddler

Child's Name Matthew Age 18 months
Observer Sara Date December 14, 1998

Check off the *areas of development* that apply:

- ❑ Shows interest in others
- ❑ Demonstrates self-awareness
- ❑ Accomplishes gross-motor milestones
- ❑ Accomplishes fine-motor milestones
- ☒ Communicates
- ❑ Acts with purpose and uses tools
- ❑ Expresses feelings

This photo, work sample and/or anecdote illustrates the following *developmental milestone(s):*

labels objects using new vocabulary

Check off whatever applies to the context of this observation:

- ☒ Child-initiated activity
- ❑ Teacher-initiated activity
- ☒ New task for this child
- ❑ Familiar task for this child
- ☒ Done independently
- ❑ Done with adult guidance
- ❑ Done with peer(s)
- ❑ Time spent (1-5 mins.)
- ☒ Time spent (5-15 mins.)
- ❑ Time spent (15+ mins.)

Anecdotal Note: Describe what you saw the child do and/or heard the child say.

Matthew walks over to the drama area and puts on a hat. He says "Poweece," and proceeds to make the sound of a siren. I ask, "Oh, you're a policeman, Matthew?" He replies, "Yes," and continues the siren-like sound.

Keeping in mind the need to focus on favorites, friends, family, and developmental milestones gives purpose to your photography and helps you manage your film and film-processing budget as well.

> Correlating Other Portfolio Items to IFSP or IEP Goals

We have designed a special collection form to be used when correlating developmental information to IFSP or IEP goals: Version #3 of the Focused Portfolios™ Developmental Milestones Collection Form. Some teachers of young children with special needs prefer to use this form exclusively when documenting children's progress and accomplishments related to these goals. In addition, they complete the Favorites, Friends, and Family Collection Forms just as suggested in this book.

On the following pages you will find samples for Austin, a child with multiple special needs, collected by Anji Persico of the West Chicago Early Childhood Program, which illustrate this approach.

Developmental Milestones Collection Form

Version #3 Preschooler

(For young children with identified special needs)

Child's Name Austin Age 4.6

Observer Anji Date 10-29-00

List the *areas of development* that apply:

Gross motor

This photo, work sample and/or anecdote illustrates the following IEP goals:

transition between cube and floor with moderate assistance at hips and prompts to his hands for correct placement

Check off whatever applies to the context of this observation:

- ☐ Child-initiated activity
- ☑ Teacher-initiated activity
- ☐ New task for this child
- ☑ Familiar task for this child
- ☐ Done independently
- ☑ Done with adult guidance
- ☐ Done with peer(s)
- ☐ Time spent (1-5 mins.)
- ☑ Time spent (5-15 mins.)
- ☐ Time spent (15+ mins.)

Anecdotal Note: Describe what you saw the child do and/or heard the child say.

When placed in a 4-point, Austin maintained the position for 1 minute. He also sidestepped with support at the hips and holding onto the table. He went the length of the table twice. Austin uses AFO's, leg extenders, and his turtle brace while walking. He is also transitioning from the cube chair to the floor when his hands are placed in the correct position and his hips are physically rotated.

Focused Portfolios™ Photo

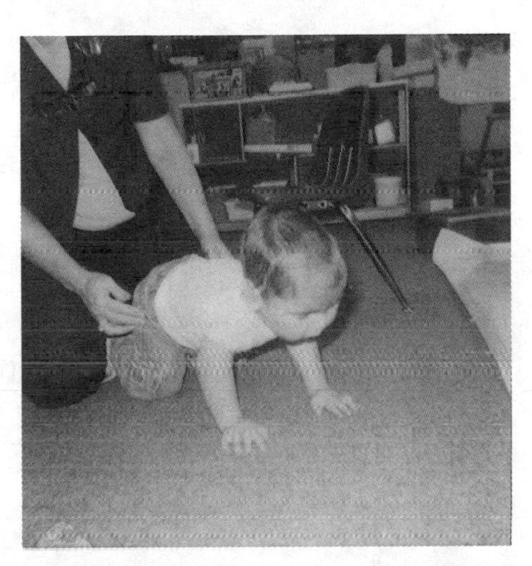

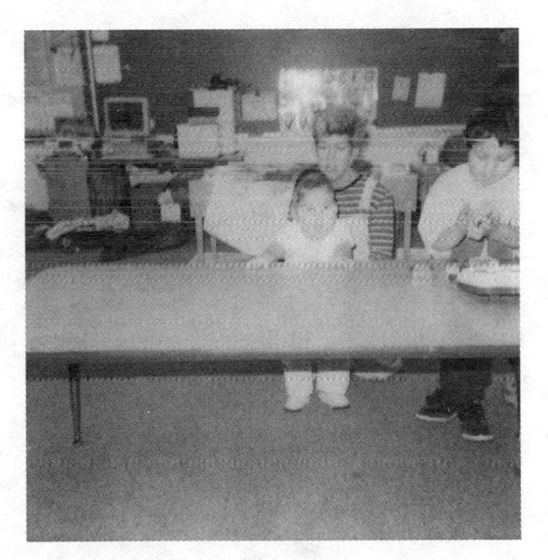

Developmental Milestones Collection Form
Version #3 Preschooler
(For young children with identified special needs)

Child's Name Austin Age 4.6
Observer Peggy Date 10-31-00

List the *areas of development* that apply:

self-help

This photo, work sample and/or anecdote illustrates the following IEP goals:

Austin will scoop when given a spoon with a prompt at the hand and wrist

Check off whatever applies to the context of this observation:

- ☐ Child-initiated activity
- ☑ Teacher-initiated activity
- ☐ New task for this child
- ☑ Familiar task for this child
- ☐ Done independently
- ☑ Done with adult guidance
- ☐ Done with peer(s)
- ☐ Time spent (1-5 mins.)
- ☒ Time spent (5-15 mins.)
- ☐ Time spent (15+ mins.)

Anecdotal Note: Describe what you saw the child do and/or heard the child say.

Austin is able to scoop with adult support at the hand and wrist. Once loaded, he is able to bring the spoon to his mouth and eat the food.

Some teachers find that they can easily correlate most of their children's special education goals to the milestones listed on the charts provided in this book. They use the Focused Portfolios™ Developmental Milestones Collection Form (Version 1). They add a sticky note that says "IEP Goal" or "IFSP Goal."

Camille Cass, a preschool teacher at the Indiana School for the Deaf, found that this system worked very well for her. She was able to correlate almost all of her children's specially identified goals directly to the milestones. And, in conferencing with family members, she preferred showing them all the typical ways in which their children were developing along with progress related to their special needs. When an IEP goal did not directly relate, Cami still used the Version 1 forms and wrote out the IEP goal on the sticky note to add to the form. See the following example for Grant.

Developmental Milestones Collection Form
Version #1 Preschooler

Child's Name Grant Age 5.2 years
Observer Camille Date 2-10-00

Check off the *areas of development* that apply:

- ☒ Thinking, Reasoning & Problem-Solving
- ❑ Emotional and Social Competency
- ❑ Gross-Motor Development
- ❑ Fine-Motor Development
- ❑ Language and Communication
- ❑ Reading & Writing Development
- ❑ Creative Development

This photo, work sample and/or anecdote illustrates the following *developmental milestone(s):*

*sustains interest in a task and works hard to solve problems independently or with some adult coaching & support
· IEP goal: uses adaptive equipment to participate in a range of activities.

Check off whatever applies to the context of this observation:

- ❑ Child-initiated activity
- ❑ Teacher-initiated activity
- ❑ New task for this child
- ☒ Familiar task for this child
- ❑ Done independently
- ❑ Done with adult guidance
- ❑ Done with peer(s)
- ❑ Time spent (1-5 mins.)
- ☒ Time spent (5-15 mins.)
- ❑ Time spent (15+ mins.)

Anecdotal Note: Describe what you saw the child do and/or heard the child say.

Grant has been working on different puzzles for 3 days. Here, Grant began to read the outline of the piece and match the piece to the same outline on the board.

Pam Giermann teaches in an inclusive preschool classroom in West Chicago. One day, while observing children's gross-motor skills on the playground, she documented a child with a disability who climbed the stairs to the top of the slide unassisted. When she got the photographs developed and reviewed her observation notes, she realized she had actually documented progress toward an existing IEP goal for this child. She attached a sticky note on which she had written "IEP Goal" to the collection form with the photos of the child in action.

chapter 5

Favorites Collection Form
Child's Name Brandon
Observer Beth
Date October 1998

> More on How to Fit Documentation into Your Busy Day

By now you may be thinking: "There is so much to plan, organize, and think about in order to get started with the Focused Portfolios™ process. How am I ever going to fit all of this in?" In this chapter, we offer tips and tools for making the process more efficient and manageable. We want you to be successful and feel good about using this assessment tool. We encourage you to pick and choose from among these suggestions. Try them out. Adapt them as needed. See what works best for you.

We have already made several recommendations regarding observation and documentation. The key to observing and recording is planning so that they become regular parts of your routine.

Planning is a complex activity and includes

- preparing materials in advance
- keeping track of observations
- sharing responsibility for observation with colleagues
- selecting optimal times to observe and record
- planning to involve the preschool children

Here are some additional timesaving tips for planning:

> Keeping Track of Observations

There are many strategies to help you keep track of observations:

- color-coding collection forms by area of development
- placing incomplete color-coded forms vertically in children's files
- checking off areas of development on white forms
- using the Recording Observations by Date Forms
- sharing responsibility for observations with colleagues
- planning to observe specific children on specific days

As part of your planning, you will want to choose from among these strategies and organize materials accordingly.

Color-Coding Developmental Milestones Collection Forms

Many teachers color-code the Developmental Milestones Collection Forms by areas of development. They choose seven colors of paper and assign a specific area to each color.

If your program chooses this option, paper can be purchased in seven different colors. If you have existing supplies, assign colors based on availability. The Favorites, Friends, and Family forms can be copied onto white or colored paper.

The benefit of color-coding is that by quickly checking each child's folder, you soon recognize which areas of development have yet to be documented by the colors of the pages, which remain blank.

Beth Hendricks at Little Rainbows Preschool in Mackinaw, Illinois, made a color-coded poster of the milestones, coordinating the colors with the same ones she had chosen for the collection forms. The poster was placed on the wall above her desk, near her crate of portfolios. In this way, she could easily learn the color-coding and study the milestones as she was filing photos and work samples.

Placing Incomplete Forms Vertically in Files

Some of the teachers in Peoria who piloted this portfolio process invented this next strategy. As they began a collection, they placed all of the blank colored pages standing upright (vertically) in each child's file. In this way the forms were sticking out of the tops of the files and could be easily seen by the teachers.

Each time they completed a collection form, they turned the page so that it was horizontal and no longer visible over the top edge. At a glance, they could see which colored forms still remained upright, and knew immediately which forms were still incomplete for each child.

Checking Off Areas of Development on White Forms

Some programs do not have sufficient money in their budgets for colored paper. Other teachers have informed us that they prefer to use white paper for all copying. We recommend that you and your colleagues choose what works best for you.

If you are using white paper for the collection forms, you can choose to prepare each child's folder in advance by placing a check mark in a different area of development on each page. Then place the prepared forms in the child's portfolio ready for writing anecdotes. When you begin your observations, you will always know which areas of development have yet to be documented because the check mark you made in advance will automatically cue you.

Some teachers do not mark the forms ahead of time, but instead have stacks of white forms located around the classroom. As they observe the children, they can easily access the forms and enter all of the necessary information at the time of documentation.

Sara Maiorano and Cynthia Brissett-Lopie at Centre de la Petite Enfance St. Mary's in Montreal used a large, three-ring notebook and divided it into sections for each child. They photocopied many blank Developmental Milestones Collection Forms on white paper and put seven of them into each section. They put blank copies of the Favorites, Friends, and Family forms at the back of the notebook for use as needed.

Using the Recording Observations by Date Forms

On the following pages are forms that we have designed to help you easily keep track of your observations by date and by area of development. *(These forms also appear in appendix A.)* One form keeps track of the group. The other tracks observations for individual children. The forms differ for infants, toddlers, and preschoolers because of the differences in the areas of development.

On the Recording Class Observations by Date Form, note the column for children's names, as well as columns for each area of development from the Developmental Milestones Charts. Beside each child's name, there is space for you to note the date when you last observed that child. You can enter more than one date in each space. You may want to post this form on a cupboard door in your classroom or on a bulletin board near your portfolio files or desk area.

The teaching team at Las Cumbres Learning Center in New Mexico used highlighter pens to color-code the areas of development on the tracking forms to correspond with the colors of the collection forms. They found this an easy way to coordinate their record of whom they had observed and whom they had not.

Cycling through the class list on this form can be a helpful way to keep track and make sure no child is missed. You want to make sure that you are recording observations on a regular basis for each child. By reading across the columns next to the child's name, you can see by the dates how much time has gone by since your last entry. You will become aware of the children on whom you focus most often and those whom you tend to miss. (If you use a different source for your milestone information, you can make your own version of this form and include the areas that are identified in that source.)

Many teachers find it helpful to keep track of what has been filed in each child's portfolio as well. Preschool teacher Marie Salas, from Springer Early Care and Education Center in New Mexico, designed a form similar to the ones on pages 133 and 134 to keep track of what she had placed in each child's individual folder.

Focused Portfolios™

Recording Class Observations by Date
Infant/Toddler

Instructions for using this form: Enter the names of all children in the group. Working across the page, write the dates of your observations in the appropriate columns.

Child's Name	Shows Interest in Others	Demonstrates Self-Awareness	Gross-Motor Development	Fine-Motor Development	Communicates	Acts with Purpose and Uses Tools	Expresses Feelings

Focused Portfolios™

Recording Class Observations by Date

Preschooler

Instructions for using this form: Enter the names of all children in the group. Working across the page, write the dates of your observations in the appropriate columns.

Child's Name	Thinking, Reasoning, and Problem Solving	Emotional and Social Competency	Language and Communication	Gross-Motor Development	Fine-Motor Development	Reading and Writing Development	Creative Development

Focused Portfolios™

Recording Individual Child Observations by Date
Infant/Toddler

Child's Name ______________________________

Instructions for using this form: Place this form on the outside of each child's portfolio folder. As you record and file observation documentation in the child's folder, write the dates of your observations in the appropriate columns.

Documentation Collected	Date(s) for Fall Collection	Date(s) for Spring Collection
Favorites		
Friends		
Family		
Shows Interest in Others		
Demonstrates Self-Awareness		
Gross-Motor Development		
Fine-Motor Development		
Communicates		
Acts with Purpose and Uses Tools		
Expresses Feelings		

Focused Portfolios™

Recording Individual Child Observations by Date
Preschoolers

Child's Name ______________________________

Instructions for using this form: Place this form on the outside of each child's portfolio folder. As you record and file observation documentation in the child's folder, write the dates of your observations in the appropriate columns.

Documentation Collected	Date(s) for Fall Collection	Date(s) for Spring Collection
Favorites		
Friends		
Family		
Thinking, Reasoning, and Problem-Solving		
Emotional and Social Competency		
Language and Communication		
Gross-Motor Development		
Fine-Motor Development		
Reading and Writing Development		
Creative Development		

Sharing Responsibility for Observation with Colleagues

If there are two or more adults in the classroom, you can prearrange a time during the day when one of you will observe and take photos. A three- to five-minute observation can give you a wealth of information about one to three children. If each of you can fit a few of these very brief times into your week, you will be able to compile a considerable amount of information (work samples, anecdotes, and photos) about each child for each collection cycle.

You may choose to split the class list and assign a specific group of children to each adult. Each of you can keep track of your groups using the Recording Class Observations by Date Form.

Many programs assign a primary caregiver to each child. This arrangement can help decide who will observe and record information about each child, keep track of what's been collected for those portfolios, and conduct the conferences with the families. However, if you see something noteworthy about any child in the group, even one for whom you are not the primary caregiver, it should at least be shared verbally with the primary caregiver. If you have the time, write an anecdote for the portfolio. This can be a shared and collaborative process.

Some teachers and assistants are not comfortable writing anecdotes. Working as a team can help make this easier. As teachers talk with each other about observations and what to document, writing skills and comfort levels may be strengthened.

Veronica Cisowski is an Anglo preschool teacher in a bilingual program in West Chicago. Veronica speaks fluent Spanish but relies on her native Spanish-speaking assistant teachers to help her as she writes her anecdotes in Spanish. She has made this commitment to record in the native language of families so they can read her observation notes in the portfolio. She and her coworkers meet at the end of each day for ten minutes or so and reflect on the children's accomplishments.

Asking a third party (another teacher or director) to read documentation and offer supportive comments may also be helpful.

Planning to Observe Specific Children on Specific Days

In order to plan ahead and make sure all the children are observed, many teachers identify small groups of children that will be observed each day. This helps them keep track and make sure they do not miss any particular child. If teachers have the same group of children for full days each week, having a "Monday Observation Group," a "Tuesday Observation Group," and so on enables them to make sure that, over time, no one is missed.

In some classrooms, each teacher has a different daily observation group. In this way, by the end of the week, each child may have at least one observation recorded.

If teachers have half-day groups, they can do the same. Because the children's attendance time is limited, they may record only one observation for each child every two weeks. Those teachers who have children who attend only two or three days a week may have to adapt this idea even further. For children who attend only two or three half days per week, teachers and assistant teachers find that one observation per child a month may be the most they can record. Accepting this and planning carefully helps teachers manage these variations in attendance. If you remember that the goal is to collect ten items of portfolio documentation across a three- to four-month period, you can figure out how best to fit in weekly and daily observations.

> Selecting Optimal Times to Observe and Record

Teachers who include observation times right in their written plans find that they are more likely to observe regularly. By using this strategy, you can look at the layout of any given day and figure out when to observe.

You do not have to step aside from your interactions with children. You can plan for observation and documentation while you are with them. For infants and toddlers, one time to plan for observation is when at least some of the children are napping. Because during nap times there are fewer children to actively supervise, you are more likely to have the opportunity to take a quick photo of any of the following:

- one or two children playing on the floor or sitting in high chairs
- a toddler drawing or playing at the water table
- an infant looking in a mirror, sitting opposite another child, or sitting in another adult's lap looking at a book
- an infant on the changing table discovering his feet or responding to a mobile suspended above

Have your camera ready and prepare a few collection forms on a clipboard or in a nearby file folder. If you have photocopied these forms for each child, and filed sets of them in advance, then select only the files of those children who are awake at the time.

For three- to five-year-old children, there are usually certain times of the day and certain activities during which they are able to manage fairly independently. The activities can be set up in advance and require neither high maintenance nor high guidance on the teachers' part. During choice time or quiet reading time, there will probably be at least one three- to five-minute segment when every child is engaged and there is no safety issue or emergency. It is then that a brief observation, carefully focused on a few children, can occur.

If adequate supervision is in place, the playground often provides good opportunities to capture gross-motor milestones, dramatic play episodes, and examples of friends and favorites. Group times or circle times frequently offer opportunities to photograph children concentrating on a storybook that is being read or engaging in music and movement. Having one adult lead these activities while another observes and records is helpful.

> Organizing Data at the End of the Day

Plan for some time when you can think back over the whole day. Making this reflection time a daily routine—as little as five to ten minutes at the end of each day—will help tremendously in accumulating more written documentation. Use a class list and try to recall and write anecdotes about as many of the children as possible. If the group is larger than eight, do this for one half or one third of the group.

If you're taking longer than ten minutes, you may want to rethink the way you are writing anecdotes. Your notes should be brief, concise descriptions of what you saw and heard. Remember to use the checklist on the collection forms to establish the context in which the child demonstrated her accomplishments. That will save a lot of time.

This daily reflection time can be another important way to share the responsibility with your teaching colleagues. Set up regular times to discuss what each of you on the teaching team is seeing the children do. Plan for regular conversation at naptime or at the end of each day to make sure this ongoing communication does not get neglected. Again, ten to fifteen minutes should be more than enough if this happens regularly. Having a class list and a Developmental Milestones Chart handy will help you keep the conversation on track and assist in sharing information about all of the children.

> Plan to Involve Preschool Children

Another way of planning for collection is to talk with the children about what you are trying to accomplish. Three-, four-, and five-year-olds can understand and participate in collecting work samples that demonstrate their abilities and skills.

Sometimes children are willing to talk about how they went about producing their work. They may say they worked a long time on something. Or they may say, "I like this one the best." After a group effort, one or two children may describe each child's role in the task. These valuable conversations provide you with words you can quote in the portfolio. They also give you insight to the child's thinking and motivation for choosing certain activities. In these discussions, you may also learn firsthand about the child's favorites and friends.

If a child expresses a desire to include a work sample in the portfolio that does not line up with one of the developmental milestones, that's fine. When children are excited about and involved in collecting documentation, it's a positive sign. These children are feeling proud of their efforts. It's appropriate to honor that pride.

Organizing forms, with or without color-coding; keeping track of observations; and involving colleagues and children are all ways to plan more efficient documentation. A few additional tips and suggestions for smooth, manageable assessment practices follow.

> Be Brief

No matter what time of day you choose to observe and document, you may or may not have the time to write a detailed anecdote. You may only be able to jot down a few words and then later add a more detailed explanation of what you saw. The key is to be sure that your brief note contains the core reason why you chose to capture this particular moment. When the main idea is captured in writing, your memory of the event is triggered, and you are able to fill in the details at a later time.

Keep in mind that if your camera is ready and you know what your focus is, then you can likely capture a moment on film and write a key phrase. This takes only a minute or two.

> When to Be Flexible

Of course, there are some days when, despite your planning, things are hectic. There is no opportunity to watch and document or take a photo. The reality of classroom life requires flexibility. If you are committed to planning the time for collection within your regular classroom routine, you will make it happen, even though on some days it will work more smoothly than on others.

After six months of working with the Focused Portfolios™ process, several teachers in the Peoria, Illinois, pilot group offered these words of advice and encouragement:

"Don't be overwhelmed by the paperwork."

"Realize it takes a while to get used to a new system, and don't be too hard on yourself."

"Do a little each day."

"You have to give it time to want to make it work. Otherwise, you won't have the desire to integrate this system into a working assessment tool."

"You'll be surprised how simple it is once you learn it."

We have found that teachers who rely on finding random time to observe and collect samples or take photos are almost always left with too few quotes and anecdotes of what children actually said and did in a situation. They find it difficult to provide a rounded, well-documented account of each child's accomplishments and progress.

chapter 6

Favorites Collection Form
Child's Name Brandon
Observer Beth
Date October 1998

> Ideas for Experienced Users and a More Complex Portfolio: Sierra

We encourage you to give yourself time to go through a complete year of collections in your program (that may be two or three collections) before making the process more complex. Use the system in the way you have learned thus far. Develop a comfort level with the collection process and with your own knowledge of the developmental milestones and the collection forms. If you are a beginner with this kind of assessment, you may want to save this chapter to read at a later date. We trust that you are in the best position to know when you are ready to take the next step.

> Setting New Goals for Yourself

Using the Focused Portfolios™ process is a work in progress. With authentic classroom assessment, there are always new aspects of development to be uncovered, more insight to be gained, and additional environmental changes to be considered.

We want to assure you that as you gain more experience with this process, you will find more strategies for making it efficient and manageable. Once you've tried out the basic approach, we're confident you'll want to adapt it to your particular setting and personal style.

In this chapter, we identify some areas that can make the Focused Portfolios™ process work more smoothly for teachers as they gain experience. These include the following:

- recording information about more than one area of development
- using other sources of developmental information
- improving your anecdotal writing
- tracking progress using multiple anecdotes

These tips can be applied one at a time, all at once, or something in between. We will go through these suggestions and then include a sample collection for Sierra that illustrates many of them.

Recording Information About More Than One Area of Development

Some teachers record information about more than one area of development on the same collection form. With experience, they have learned and internalized the milestones charts and can identify more than one area of development and several milestones in one observation.

They

- mark the primary area of development with an X
- list the related developmental milestones in the appropriate spaces
- identify additional areas of development that were evident and mark with a check mark
- add other related milestones below the previous ones

This gives more detailed information in preparing for reflection and sharing with families. Here is an example of a Developmental Milestones Collection Form with several areas of development and milestones noted.

Developmental Milestones Collection Form
Version #1 Preschooler

Child's Name Brent Age 5
Observer Sonya Date 8/19/98

Check off the *areas of development* that apply:

- ☑ Thinking, Reasoning & Problem-Solving
- ❑ Emotional and Social Competency
- ❑ Gross-Motor Development
- ☑ Fine-Motor Development
- ☑ Language and Communication
- ❑ Reading & Writing Development
- ☒ Creative Development

This photo, work sample and/or anecdote illustrates the following *developmental milestone(s):*

includes details in artwork; experiments with materials + finds challenging ways to use them; uses complex sentence structure; builds 3-D block structures

Check off whatever applies to the context of this observation:

- ☒ Child-initiated activity
- ❑ Teacher-initiated activity
- ❑ New task for this child
- ❑ Familiar task for this child
- ❑ Done independently
- ☒ Done with adult guidance
- ❑ Done with peer(s)
- ❑ Time spent (1-5 mins.)
- ❑ Time spent (5-15 mins.)
- ☒ Time spent (15+ mins.)

Anecdotal Note: Describe what you saw the child do and/or heard the child say.

Brent made a sculpture of wood & fabric using glue to hold it together. I asked him to tell me about it. He said, "I wrapped this all around [referring to some black lacy fabric] and I glued them and I painted some of this. And that's about it. Oh, and one part broke," he said as he showed it to me.

If you look at the samples earlier in the book, you will see that the teachers did not check off more than one area of development. But, on close examination, you can see that they easily could have. Teachers often focus their observation and documentation on one area and find that, upon reflection, they're able to see many more in evidence. Marking more than one can be done at the time of initial recording, or at a later time, after reflecting upon the anecdote and photo or work sample. Either way, you are recognizing that young children often show us their skills and abilities in rich, integrated ways. Your documentation can reflect that richness, and recognize and celebrate all that a child can do.

In the sample collection later in this chapter, Sierra's teacher did check off more than one area on most of her collection forms.

Using Other Sources of Developmental Information

You can deepen and refine documentation, as well as your own knowledge, by incorporating child development checklists and charts obtained from other sources. You either add more developmental information to the collection forms or deepen the developmental descriptions within your anecdotes.

Some teachers use the High/Scope Key Experiences as the framework for their curriculum. When they write anecdotal comments that incorporate the Key Experiences, it serves to enrich and tie together the processes of assessment and curriculum planning. *(See the Developmental Milestones Collection Form for Shannon on page 64.)*

Teachers of infants and toddlers who wish to document more fully the growing motor skills of the children in their classrooms may turn to other sources for more specific descriptions of physical development. One choice might be to use the Assessment, Evaluation and Programming System (AEPS). *(See the Developmental Milestones Collection Form for Charisse on page 63.)*

In appendix C, we include additional samples of documentation showing how other developmental milestones sources have been used. In appendix E, we give reference information. If you are considering adding more developmental information to your own observations, you can review the reference list and samples there.

Improving Your Anecdotal Writing—Going Beyond the Basics

Writing an anecdote that fully captures the incident you observed is not an easy task. As an experienced user, you may wish to consider the following two suggestions.

Engage in Self-Critique and Editing Expand the amount of information you write in anecdotes by including more details. For example, add contextual information such as the child's approach to beginning or ending a task.

Here's how you might approach this. Read over the anecdotes you've written in past collections. As you review them, ask yourself if there are details that you remember but didn't write about a child's behavior. Can you recall any interaction in a situation that might have been helpful to include? Think about how you might have developed each anecdote more fully.

Here are two examples of anecdotes: one with few, contextual details, and the other more fully developed. The first anecdote has few details. It was written for the first collection.

"Kyle is able to climb on our outdoor play equipment."

With a goal of improving her anecdotal writing, the teacher reviewed the former anecdote and edited it as follows:

"Kyle (four years old) climbs on the slide and the jungle gym outside. He hangs from the bars by his knees, and asks me to push him back and forth. To get down, he comes to a sitting position and lowers himself to the ground by himself."

You can apply these editing strategies to all future anecdotes that you write. As you complete your observation, if time permits, review and edit what you have written. See if there are other pieces of information or direct quotes that you could include. If there isn't time in the moment, revisit the anecdote later with the same purpose in mind. As an experienced user, you further increase your accountability, to yourself and to others, by developing the ability to write more detailed records of children's growth and learning.

Strive for Objectivity in Your Anecdotes Another way to improve written observations is to check for objectivity in the words you have chosen. Once again, review some of your anecdotes from past collections. Identify any words that imply judgments about what children have done or that include subjective comments such as "John really likes to . . ." or "Brenda enjoys playing with . . ." Teachers may draw conclusions about children's likes and dislikes, but they cannot know for certain what a child "likes" or "enjoys" unless the child tells them so.

If you can quote John saying, "I really like to smash playdough," you are writing a factual anecdote. However, if you think that John likes playdough because he plays with it often, invites his friends to join him, and stays at the activity for long periods of time, we recommend that you objectively list those facts rather than writing your conclusion.

We recognize that teachers do draw conclusions about children's behavior. Making judgments is part of evaluation and belongs in the reflection and planning process. Objective anecdotes provide the data that allows you to make informed conclusions. It is premature to form judgments as you write observations.

An informative, factual anecdote tells

- what the child did
- what the child said
- what you saw
- what you heard

An informative factual anecdote does not tell what you thought or felt about the incident.

Tracking Children's Progress

You can use the collection forms to track the same behavior or cluster of skills in one area of development. Over the course of several months, write a series of anecdotes on the same collection form. Each anecdote describes how the child is using and refining the same cluster of skills or behaviors. To show the time period involved, be sure to write the date next to each anecdote. Accompanying work samples and photographs illustrate the level of engagement and the child's ability to apply her skills. On the following page is an example of multiple anecdotes pertaining to one area of development written on a Developmental Milestones Collection Form.

Developmental Milestones Collection Form
Version #1 Infant/Toddler

Child's Name Tyrell Age 7 months
Observer Sharon Date 2/12/99

Check off the *areas of development* that apply:

- ❑ Shows interest in others
- ☑ Demonstrates self-awareness
- ❑ Accomplishes gross-motor milestones
- ❑ Accomplishes fine-motor milestones
- ❑ Communicates
- ❑ Acts with purpose and uses tools
- ❑ Expresses feelings

This photo, work sample and/or anecdote illustrates the following *developmental milestone(s):*

- smiles and interacts with self in mirror
- identifies one or more body parts

Check off whatever applies to the context of this observation:

- ❑ Child-initiated activity
- ☑ Teacher-initiated activity
- ☑ New task for this child
- ❑ Familiar task for this child
- ❑ Done independently
- ☑ Done with adult guidance
- ❑ Done with peer(s)
- ❑ Time spent (1-5 mins.)
- ☑ Time spent (5-15 mins.)
- ❑ Time spent (15+ mins.)

Anecdotal Note: Describe what you saw the child do and/or heard the child say.
When Tyrell is placed on the mat near the mirror, he turns his head toward the mirror and looks carefully at his reflection.

3/5/99 (8 mos.) - I placed Tyrell next to the mirror. At first I was beside him so both our reflections were in the mirror. Then, very slowly, I placed a light blanket over Ty's head and called out: "Where's Ty?" He pulled the blanket away from his head, squealed loudly and slapped his palm against the mirror. When we repeated this game Ty responded in the same way each time, giggling as I came close with the blanket.

5/7/99 (10 mos) - Tyrell, Justin and Camille were all on the rug. I was singing "Head, Shoulders, Knees and Toes". Each time I sang "Head", Tyrell put his hands on his head. Tyrell watched me closely, still holding his hands on his head, as I sang the rest of the song and did the accompanying actions.

If a photo had accompanied the initial anecdote about Tyrell, there would not have been room on the Developmental Milestones Collection Form to write this series of anecdotes. On the next page is a form designed to make it easier to record many related anecdotes about the same child. *(This form also appears in appendix A.)*

Tracking Progress through Multiple Anecdotes

Child's Name ________________ Area of Development ________________

Anecdotal Note: Describe what you saw the child do and/or heard the child say.

Date:__________ Child's age__________ Observer______________

Anecdotal Note: Describe what you saw the child do and/or heard the child say.

Date:__________ Child's age__________ Observer______________

Anecdotal Note: Describe what you saw the child do and/or heard the child say.

Date:__________ Child's age__________ Observer______________

The initial observation anecdote is written on the Developmental Milestones Collection Form, and is accompanied by a photo, if there is one. Any additional anecdotes related to the same developmental information can be written on this new form and stapled to the Developmental Milestones Collection Form.

Sierra's Collection

On the following pages is a sample portfolio collection for Sierra. You will see that Sierra's teacher, Linda Desroches, used many of the suggestions we have just shared. Look through this collection and note the way the forms are filled out. Read the anecdotes and look at the photographs. Check out the milestones identified and match them back up to the descriptions of Sierra's actions. Use this sample as a learning tool when you are ready to add more complexity to the collection process.

We are grateful to Linda and to Sierra and her family for sharing with us. They have given teachers a valuable resource.

Favorites Collection Form

Child's Name Sierra Date April '99

Observer Linda

After observing the child on multiple occasions, describe a favorite activity that the child does often. Add details that you've noticed about the child's interests and choices. Add a photo if you can.

Description: A favorite activity for Sierra is doll play. She goes to the pretend sink, cups her hands under the faucet, then rubs her hands over the doll's head. She unfolds a cloth, and wraps the doll inside it. On other occasions, she will rock the doll and sing softly to it. She uses spoons and bottles to feed the dolls and does the snaps and buttons on their clothes.

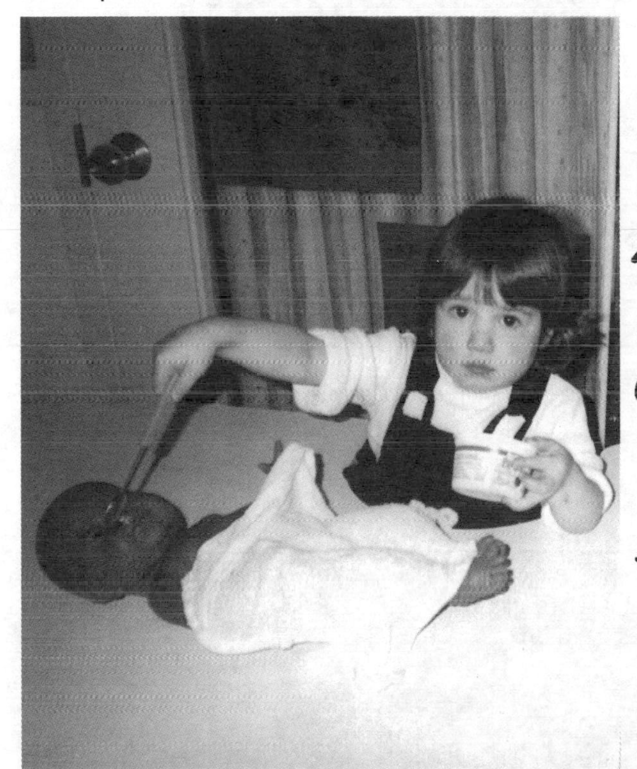

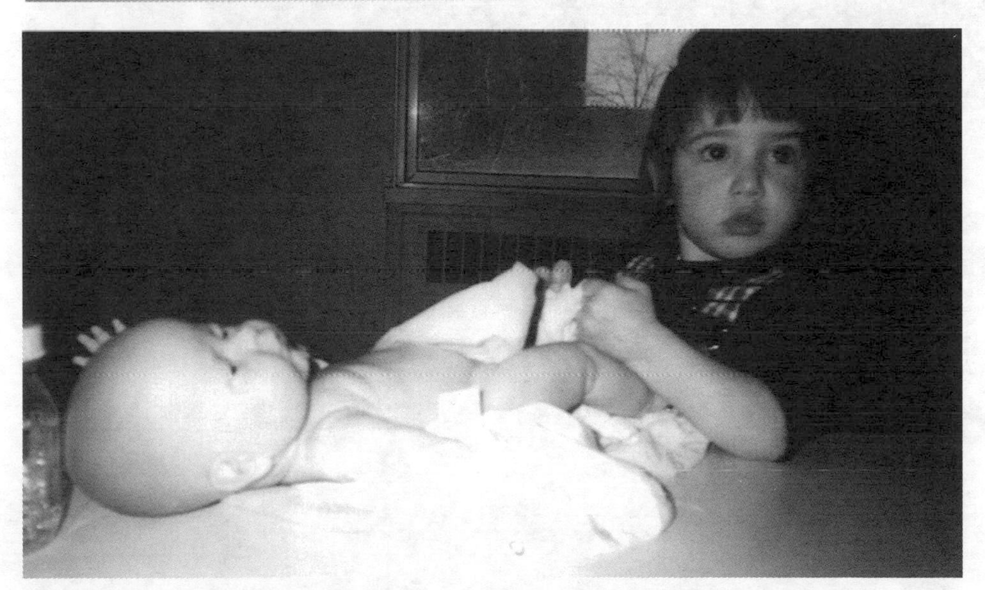

Friends Collection Form

Child's Name Sierra Date May '99

Observer Linda

Based on your observations, who are this child's friends? What do they do together? How does this child express his or her feelings towards them? Add a photo to illustrate this friendship.

Description: Each day, Sierra spends much of her time interacting with other children. She has progressed from simply observing another child (as she is here with Rebecca) to playing <u>with</u> them.

Family Collection Form

Child's Name Sierra Date April 1999

Observer Linda

Families often have stories to share about their child's accomplishments at home. They also have special moments with their child in your classroom. Use this form to document a story that the child's family has shared with you, or take a photo of a special moment between the child and the people who are important in his or her life.

Description: On a family trip to Santa's Village, Sierra played in the building blocks with Mom.

Developmental Milestones Collection Form
Version #1 Infant/Toddler

Child's Name Sierra Age 20 months

Observer Linda Date Feb., 1999

Check off the *areas of development* that apply:

* ☒ Shows interest in others
- ☑ Demonstrates self-awareness
- ☐ Accomplishes gross-motor milestones
- ☐ Accomplishes fine-motor milestones
- ☑ Communicates
- ☑ Acts with purpose and uses tools
- ☐ Expresses feelings

This photo, work sample and/or anecdote illustrates the following *developmental milestone(s):*

demonstrates interest in what other children are doing; creates long babbled sentences; says 2 or 3 clear words; puts on simple garments; plays pretend

Check off whatever applies to the context of this observation:

- ☒ Child-initiated activity
- ☐ Teacher-initiated activity
- ☐ New task for this child
- ☐ Familiar task for this child
- ☒ Done independently
- ☐ Done with adult guidance
- ☒ Done with peer(s)
- ☐ Time spent (1-5 mins.)
- ☐ Time spent (5-15 mins.)
- ☐ Time spent (15+ mins.)

Anecdotal Note: Describe what you saw the child do and/or heard the child say.

Sierra took a baby doll in her arms and rocked it from side to side. She then got a soft material book from the book shelf, opened the pages and wrapped the baby in the book. She called out and pointed to Anissah. Anissah picked up a smaller doll and sat beside Sierra.

(see April example attached)

Focused Portfolios™ Photo

On several occasions this week, Sierra approached other children to help put on shoes, slippers or rubber boots. At these times, she looked at them, babbled a string of unintelligible words, and clearly said the word, "shoes."

Developmental Milestones Collection Form
Version #1 Infant/Toddler

Child's Name Sierra

Age 23 months

Observer Linda

Date May '99

Check off the *areas of development* that apply:

- ☑ Shows interest in others
- * ☒ Demonstrates self-awareness
- ☑ Accomplishes gross-motor milestones
- ❑ Accomplishes fine-motor milestones
- ☑ Communicates
- ❑ Acts with purpose and uses tools
- ☑ Expresses feelings

This photo, work sample and/or anecdote illustrates the following *developmental milestone(s):*

shows strong sense of self; exhibits satisfaction in presence of familiar adults; runs with ease; says 2 or 3 clear words; uses words to express some feelings

Check off whatever applies to the context of this observation:

- ❑ Child-initiated activity
- ☒ Teacher-initiated activity
- ❑ New task for this child
- ❑ Familiar task for this child
- ❑ Done independently
- ❑ Done with adult guidance
- ❑ Done with peer(s)
- ❑ Time spent (1-5 mins.)
- ❑ Time spent (5-15 mins.)
- ❑ Time spent (15+ mins.)

Anecdotal Note: Describe what you saw the child do and/or heard the child say.

When I told Sierra that nap would be in a few minutes, she looked at me, said, "No!" and continued playing. When I tried to hand her a cup with water, again she said, "No!" and ran to the corner of the room. I caught up with her, tickled her, and she had a good nap.

If another child tries to take a toy that she is using, she hugs the toy tightly to her chest, looks at the other child and loudly says, "Mine!"

Developmental Milestones Collection Form
Version #1 Infant/Toddler

Child's Name Sierra Age 20 months
Observer Linda Date Feb. '99

Check off the *areas of development* that apply:

- [x] Shows interest in others
- [ ] Demonstrates self-awareness
- [x] Accomplishes gross-motor milestones *
- [ ] Accomplishes fine-motor milestones
- [ ] Communicates
- [x] Acts with purpose and uses tools
- [ ] Expresses feelings

This photo, work sample and/or anecdote illustrates the following *developmental milestone(s):*

walks with ease
begins to walk up and down stairs

Check off whatever applies to the context of this observation:

- [x] Child-initiated activity
- [ ] Teacher-initiated activity
- [ ] New task for this child
- [ ] Familiar task for this child
- [ ] Done independently
- [ ] Done with adult guidance
- [x] Done with peer(s)
- [ ] Time spent (1-5 mins.)
- [x] Time spent (5-15 mins.)
- [ ] Time spent (15+ mins.)

Anecdotal Note: Describe what you saw the child do and/or heard the child say.

When Sierra noticed that the wooden steps were out, she clapped her hands and danced, saying "Yay!" She walked up the steps alternating feet. She jumped down, over one step, and landed on her feet. She jumped many times (maybe 10?). When offered help by an adult, Sierra replied, "No, self," as she proudly jumped down, laughing and saying, "Yay!"

Tracking Progress through Multiple Anecdotes

Child's Name Sierra Area of Development Gross Motor

Anecdotal Note: Describe what you saw the child do and/or heard the child say.

Date: April '99 Child's age 22 mos. Observer Linda

Now, Sierra walks up the stairs of the climbing structure with confidence and stability. When crossing the bridge, she no longer focuses on the equipment, but rather, looks down and calls to the teachers, runs across, and interacts with other children or goes down the slide.

(see photo attached)

Anecdotal Note: Describe what you saw the child do and/or heard the child say.

Date:________ Child's age________ Observer________

Anecdotal Note: Describe what you saw the child do and/or heard the child say.

Date:________ Child's age________ Observer________

Focused Portfolios™ Photo

Developmental Milestones Collection Form
Version #1 Infant/Toddler

Child's Name Sierra Age 21 months
Observer Linda Date March 99

Check off the *areas of development* that apply:

- ❑ Shows interest in others
- ☑ Demonstrates self-awareness
- ❑ Accomplishes gross-motor milestones
- * ☒ Accomplishes fine-motor milestones
- ❑ Communicates
- ❑ Acts with purpose and uses tools
- ❑ Expresses feelings

This photo, work sample and/or anecdote illustrates the following *developmental milestone(s):*

scribbles with marker
draws circles
explores everything

Check off whatever applies to the context of this observation:

- ❑ Child-initiated activity
- ☒ Teacher-initiated activity
- ☒ New task for this child
- ❑ Familiar task for this child
- ☒ Done independently
- ❑ Done with adult guidance
- ❑ Done with peer(s)
- ❑ Time spent (1-5 mins.)
- ☒ Time spent (5-15 mins.)
- ❑ Time spent (15+ mins.)

Anecdotal Note: Describe what you saw the child do and/or heard the child say.

Sierra chooses to use markers or to paint with paintbrushes more frequently now than before. She observes what happens when she moves a sponge brush or plastic cars through the paint. In the attached drawing, she used many colors of markers and made various types of strokes.

Sierra

Developmental Milestones Collection Form
Version #1 Infant/Toddler

Child's Name Sierra Age On going

Observer Linda Date May '99

Check off the *areas of development* that apply:

- ❑ Shows interest in others
- ❑ Demonstrates self-awareness
- ☑ Accomplishes gross-motor milestones
- ❑ Accomplishes fine-motor milestones
- * ☒ Communicates
- ❑ Acts with purpose and uses tools
- ❑ Expresses feelings

This photo, work sample and/or anecdote illustrates the following *developmental milestone(s):*

Says some clear words; labels objects using new vocabulary; tiptoes; creates long babbled sentences

Check off whatever applies to the context of this observation:

❑ Child-initiated activity	❑ Done with adult guidance
❑ Teacher-initiated activity	❑ Done with peer(s)
❑ New task for this child	❑ Time spent (1-5 mins.)
❑ Familiar task for this child	❑ Time spent (5-15 mins.)
❑ Done independently	❑ Time spent (15+ mins.)

Anecdotal Note: Describe what you saw the child do and/or heard the child say.

See attached word list and anecdotes.

Infant/Toddler Word List

Child Sierra Teacher(s) Linda & Audrey

Date:	Word Approximations, Words and/or Word Combinations	Context (imitation, response to comment or question, self-initiated)
Oct. '98	"ook, ook" (look, look)	
" "	"mama" "daddy"	whenever she sees them
Dec. '98	"bye-bye"	when Mom or Dad leaves in the a.m.
Feb. '99	"doggie"	on neighborhood walks
March '99	"up"	when she wants to be picked up
" "	"boots" "shoes"	
" "	"Yay!"	to show pleasure
April '99	"tuck" (truck)	
" "	"Kitty"	when she sees a squirrel in the yard
" "	"sit down"	
May '99	"peek-a-boo"	when playing with teachers
" "	"MINE"	

Anecdotal Comments:

Tracking Progress through Multiple Anecdotes

Child's Name Sierra Area of Development Communicates

Anecdotal Note: Describe what you saw the child do and/or heard the child say.

Date: Feb. '99 Child's age 20 mos. Observer Linda

When Sierra saw me bringing a tray into the room and placing it on the table, she walked around the table to where the tray was set and put both arms up. She went on her tippy-toes and babbled to me. She pointed her finger up and babbled more.

Anecdotal Note: Describe what you saw the child do and/or heard the child say.

Date: May '99 Child's age 23 mos. Observer Linda

Sierra's brother came to visit his sister and took his shoes off before entering the room. Sierra saw that he had done so and sat down, saying "oes," "oes." She was wearing her slippers at the time. When her brother left 20 mins. later, Sierra took her slippers off and said "oes," "oes" again. She also asked for mother, repeating "Mama" sereval times. (Her Mom stopped by & gave her a hug.)

Anecdotal Note: Describe what you saw the child do and/or heard the child say.

Date:______ Child's age______ Observer______

Developmental Milestones Collection Form
Version #1 Infant/Toddler

Child's Name Sierra Age 19 months
Observer Linda Date Feb. '99

Check off the *areas of development* that apply:

- ☐ Shows interest in others
- ☐ Demonstrates self-awareness
- ☐ Accomplishes gross-motor milestones
- ☐ Accomplishes fine-motor milestones
- ☐ Communicates
- * ☒ Acts with purpose and uses tools
- ☑ Expresses feelings

This photo, work sample and/or anecdote illustrates the following *developmental milestone(s):*

helps dress and undress self; acts to make things happen; explores objects through touch; shows pride & pleasure in accomplishments

Check off whatever applies to the context of this observation:

- ☒ Child-initiated activity
- ☐ Teacher-initiated activity
- ☐ New task for this child
- ☒ Familiar task for this child
- ☒ Done independently
- ☐ Done with adult guidance
- ☐ Done with peer(s)
- ☐ Time spent (1-5 mins.)
- ☐ Time spent (5-15 mins.)
- ☐ Time spent (15+ mins.)

Anecdotal Note: Describe what you saw the child do and/or heard the child say.

Feb. 1st We put the rhythm instruments out today and invited children to explore them. Sierra found all the bells, sat down, and took several tries to place them successfully on her ankles and wrists. She wiggled and laughed as the bells rang.

April 23rd Sierra is almost always involved in dressing and undressing routines. She takes off her shoes, socks, hats and mittens, and does so with dress-up and doll clothes as well.

Developmental Milestones Collection Form
Version #1 Infant/Toddler

Child's Name Sierra   Age 21 months
Observer Linda   Date March '99

Check off the *areas of development* that apply:

- ☑ Shows interest in others
- ☑ Demonstrates self-awareness
- ❑ Accomplishes gross-motor milestones
- ❑ Accomplishes fine-motor milestones
- ☑ Communicates
- ❑ Acts with purpose and uses tools
- * ☒ Expresses feelings

This photo, work sample and/or anecdote illustrates the following *developmental milestone(s):*

expresses feelings mostly through behavior; shows strong sense of self; says 2 or 3 clear words; shows pride & pleasure in production & creation

Check off whatever applies to the context of this observation:

- ❑ Child-initiated activity
- ❑ Teacher-initiated activity
- ❑ New task for this child
- ❑ Familiar task for this child
- ❑ Done independently
- ❑ Done with adult guidance
- ❑ Done with peer(s)
- ❑ Time spent (1-5 mins.)
- ❑ Time spent (5-15 mins.)
- ❑ Time spent (15+ mins.)

Anecdotal Note: Describe what you saw the child do and/or heard the child say.

Sierra expresses her feelings by pulling our arms to be held, clapping, crying and throwing her arms up in the air. She is combining these actions with a few key words that tell us about her feelings ("Mama!" "No" "Yay!"). Simply observing her facial expressions tells us so much about how she feels.

(see photo attached)

Focused Portfolios™ Photo

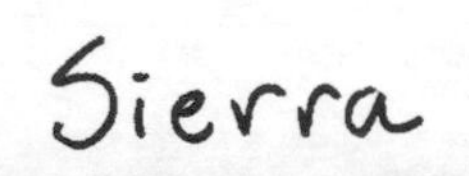

Focused Portfolios™ Reflection and Planning Form
Final Collection

Child's Name Sierra Age 23 mos. Teacher Linda Date May '99

Teacher Reflection

Refer to all *areas of development* and to the items in the portfolio

Summarize information from Favorites, Friends, and Family:

Sierra will try just about anything at the center, but she does love to play with dolls! She is gentle, nurturing and dresses and undresses them. She is showing increasing interest in other children and can be helpful to them. She particularly enjoys when you are able to visit the classroom!

List milestones accomplished:

- explores objects through touch
- picks up smaller objects easily
- identifies some body parts
- walks with ease
- moves around objects
- shows pride
- expresses feelings through behavior rather than words
- creates long, babbled sentences
- plays pretend

Describe progress observed as compared to previous collection(s):

- helps dress and undress self and dolls
- draws circles
- demonstrates interest in what other children are doing
- shows strong sense of self ("No", "Mine")
- walks up and down stairs
- says some clear words

Milestones that this child is working on:

- labels objects using new vocabulary
- combines words in 2-3 word sentences and commands

General Comments about This Child's Growth and Development Over the Course of the Year

Teacher: Sierra has progressed in so many ways: dressing and undressing, climbing, walking and running. And, she certainly knows her own wishes and is clear about communicating them.

Her vocabulary expands almost daily. We hear more clear words and some 2 word combinations. We believe this growth will continue rapidly in her 2 year old year. We know you converse with her extensively and encourage you to continue.

We'll miss Sierra as she heads to the Toddler Room in the fall. We're glad we'll still see her regularly at the center!

Family member(s):

Thanks for reminding us that Sierra's use of "no" and "mine" are a positive sign of her development. Sometimes that's hard to remember.

We've noticed so many accomplishments for Sierra. We're so proud of her. She will miss you too. It's been a terrific year for all of us.

Thanks again,

John & Diana

chapter 7

Favorites Collection Form
Child's Name Brandon
Observer Beth
Date October 1998

> Using Observations to Plan Individualized Curriculum

You're busy observing children, documenting what you see in photos, anecdotes, and work samples. But gathering information is only part of the assessment process. You must apply the information on a daily basis to enhance each child's growth and development. In this chapter, you will find ideas about planning for individual children that you incorporate as you get used to collecting documentation. At the end of the chapter will be suggestions for ways to go even further with your planning as you become more experienced at using this portfolio process.

A teacher's job is to continually select activities and experiences and, based on observations of children, to plan for curriculum that will

- support children in their present development
- extend their interests and passions
- challenge them to practice and achieve milestone behaviors and skills
- let them know you enjoy them and want them to reach their own unique potential

Using the observation notes, photos, and work samples collected for favorites, friends, family, and developmental milestones, teachers individualize curriculum. They recognize children's capabilities, personality traits, and approaches to learning. They interpret what they are seeing, and make judgments about ways to help children continue in their successes and be supported in their struggles.

This process has several steps and does not necessarily happen overnight, however. Many teachers report that, initially, it takes time to learn the process of combining skillful observation with anecdote writing. It also takes time to establish a routine of recording and filing observations. They may pay closer attention to selecting the form to use and deciding exactly what to write, than to making curricular decisions based on their observations. That's a very common scenario as teachers learn a new format. As their comfort level with the portfolio process grows, they become aware that their knowledge about each child is indeed growing. As that happens, they see that there are many ways to apply that knowledge in day-to-day routines and activities with the children.

Maria York, a preschool teacher in Streeter, Illinois, summed up the reasons why this process helps her know more about the children in her program:

"I know my children better because I observe it, take a picture of it, write it down. Then the pictures come back, and I revisit it again. So how many times have I looked at the same situation? That's why I know so much."

> Three Opportunities to Use Observation Information

There are three opportunities to use the information you have gained through observation in planning for individualized curriculum:

- spontaneously, at the time of observation
- in ongoing review, as you organize and file your documentation
- in reflection, as you periodically review what you have completed in the portfolio collection so far

Spontaneous Curriculum Planning

Teachers are intuitive people who tend to be very sensitive to the needs of others. More than likely, you have chosen the field of early care and education because you feel rewarded when you can meet children's needs. Every time you watch children (whether writing down that observation or not), you are interpreting what you see in relation to their needs and making decisions about what you will do. You may choose to act on those decisions at the time of observation by stepping in and helping the child, by holding back to see if the child can do it alone, by asking an open-ended question, or by providing a new material or activity.

These are all curricular decisions. There wasn't time to write out a plan with formal objectives. Yet you assessed how best to support a child's learning, and then acted spontaneously, in response to what you saw the child do or heard the child say.

Lydia's Story Lydia looks around her classroom of three-year-olds and sees that children are actively engaged and the classroom is running smoothly. Because things are calm, Lydia decides to observe Andre and Joel, who are wearing firefighter hats and building with blocks. She gets their portfolio folders out so that she can observe them and write documentation. In her mind, she's thinking that these two often play together. Therefore, she takes out the Friends Collection Form and writes her observations there.

She can hear the boys' comments as they build, and writes down as many as she can. Spontaneously, she makes a curricular decision: She will show support for the boys' engagement and cooperation. She moves closer to them, asking, "What are you all building here?" "A fire truck!" they respond simultaneously. Lydia wants to recognize and celebrate their work and says to them, "Wow, I can see you used a lot of blocks and had to work really hard together."

Seth's Story Eighteen-month-old Liam's mom has been away on a business trip for a few days. Today, Seth, his teacher, observes that Liam is less animated, moving more slowly and interacting less with his fellow toddlers than usual. Seth makes a mental note to write this down later, thinking he may connect it to Liam's family collection or to the documentation of one of Liam's developmental milestones, awareness of others. Seth makes a decision to intervene with Liam. He goes over and asks him, "Liam, are you missing your mom? Would you like your Teddy to make you feel better?" As Liam slowly nods, Seth takes his hand and walks him to his cubby to get his Teddy.

Beth Hendricks of Mackinaw, Illinois, reported that the pace of her teaching slowed as she used this portfolio process. She felt that her focus in the past had been following her written plans and making sure that every child completed all of the activities. After using the Focused Portfolios™ system, she found herself paying much more attention to how each child went about doing activities rather than completing them.

Ongoing Review

As you organize and file your documentation for the portfolio, you will have a ready-made opportunity to think about each child. Take advantage of this time. Classroom planning is better when teachers step back and think about what they have witnessed children actually doing. As you review photographs, work samples, and anecdotes that you have collected, and decide where in the portfolio they might go, you will see patterns in children's behaviors. As you note what their favorites are, you will learn which activities they choose often and which they tend to avoid. As you see whom they consistently choose as friends in play or at snack time, you will gain a greater sense of their current social skills. As you organize developmental milestones information, you will see areas that may be stronger than others.

The patterns in children's behavior are the key to future planning. Together with your knowledge of child development and your experience with young children, you use what you are learning about these patterns in your activity planning for the classroom.

Nellie's Story In Nellie's bilingual (English and Spanish) preschool classroom, Antonio often plays in the dramatic play area, dressing in costumes and acting out a variety of scenes. He invites other children to join in and assigns them roles, sometimes even giving them their "lines" to say. Other children go along with him, and long stories are acted out. Nellie has written a few anecdotes describing these scenarios. One afternoon as she was organizing her portfolios, she looked over her notes about Antonio and realized that she had enough documentation to demonstrate that his favorite was dramatic play. She took the sticky notes on which she had written her observations and placed them on the Favorites Collection Form.

Not all of the children in Nellie's class were joining in dramatic play in this way. So Nellie decided to have Antonio help her engage other children in that area. She discussed her plan with her teaching assistants, and, periodically, they encouraged Antonio to invite a more reluctant child into the play. In each instance, Antonio would smile broadly and say "Sure!" as he went off to gather his recruits. Some children responded to his invitations, and some did not.

Jeff's Story As Jeff organized the portfolios for his four- and five-year-olds in a program for at-risk children, he realized that he had no documentation about children's fine-motor skills. He had an art center in his classroom, well stocked with scissors and paper and a variety of sizes of markers, crayons, and pencils, as well as paint brushes. It became clear that the children in his group were not spending much time there. He decided to make some changes that might entice the children to try out tools and materials that would show him how their fine-motor skills were developing.

Jeff emptied the water table and substituted paper scraps, magazines, scissors, and hole punchers. The next day, he announced to the children that there was a change in the room and challenged them to see if they could find it. When they did, he modeled for them ways they could use the materials at the water table and took suggestions for new names for this area (since water was no longer the main ingredient!). Jeff succeeded in generating children's interest and was able to focus on the children who visited the new "Cutting and Punching Table" so that he could document their growing fine-motor skills.

Periodically Reflecting on Portfolio Items

As you review items in the portfolio collection, the patterns discussed above will become even more evident. You may choose to do your reflection separately from organizing and filing to avoid distraction. Taking the opportunity to reflect on completed portfolio items may give you a fuller picture of a child's strengths, interests, and areas of competence, as well as areas that are still in the process of developing.

Periodic review of items collected so far in each portfolio helps you to continually adapt your planning in ways that are best for each child. Regular reflection also reminds you of the areas you have, and have not, documented for each child. These practices will help you stay on top of the process of portfolio collection, as well as enable you to individualize curricular planning.

Sharon's Story As Sharon reviewed her infant/toddler portfolio collections after a month or so, she noted that she had no documentation related to the area of development "Communicates." Sharon thought for a moment and realized that promoting this area is not one of her strengths. She discussed this with her assistants and then made specific plans to interact with children so they all could watch and record communication. After two weeks, Sharon reviewed the portfolios again and saw that she now had documentation describing almost every child's communication.

Pat's Story Pat was preparing for a case conference with fellow Head Start staff. The child to be discussed was John, a four-year-old with serious language delays. As she looked at the photographs and read through her observation notes on his Favorites Collection Form, as well as on his Developmental Milestones Collection Forms, she noticed that, in each situation described, John was playing or working alone or with an adult. As she thought back over the last few weeks with John, she realized that he did not interact with other children. Sometimes she did see him watching others at play, but never joining in. She wondered if his problems with communication were inhibiting his social development. She thought about coaching strategies for helping John learn how to play alongside another child. She determined to make more of an effort to help him move toward entering a play situation in which one or more children were involved.

> Making Curricular Decisions

No matter when you review the information gained through observation, you have choices to make about your response. Will you support the child in his interests, choices, and capabilities? If so, how? Will you extend activities that the child initiates and build upon her current interests? Or will you provide just the right amount of challenge to lead him to develop new interests, make different choices, or go further in his skills?

There are endless possibilities for planning in which teachers can make adjustments for individual children. Here are three main categories:

- Supporting, Enjoying, and Celebrating Children's Choices and Capabilities
- Extending Interests
- Offering Challenge

Supporting, Enjoying, and Celebrating Children's Choices and Capabilities

Children do not grow and change in a vacuum. They need caring adults around them to support their growth. Supporting children involves assuring them that they are accepted just as they are, laughing with them not at them, enjoying their personalities and talents, and celebrating their accomplishments, no matter how small. To support children's growth and development, teachers provide age-appropriate furniture and materials and carefully plan songs, finger plays, stories, and activities they know are of interest to their age group. They build on each child's unique interests, and work with individual personality traits and developmental capabilities.

Supporting children involves nurturing them and earning their trust. Through their support, teachers communicate their unwavering faith that each child will continue to grow and learn.

There are a wide variety of teacher behaviors that could be described as "Teacher Support." These options may differ slightly depending on the age of the child. In the following table, suggestions for teacher support are divided into age categories. The ideas in this table are by no means exhaustive. You may be able to think of many other ways to provide teacher support.

Providing support to children can happen spontaneously, or it can be planned for after organizing and filing portfolio information, or after reflecting upon what's been documented so far. Here are examples of each of these ways of supporting children.

Doug's Story Doug observed preschoolers Maria, Josie, and Peng playing in the dramatic play area. "Let's go camping," suggested Josie. Doug decided to get a notepad and pen, and sat in a chair a short distance away from the children. As they enacted their camping trip, Doug wrote down their words as best as he could.

Later, at circle time, Doug led the children in a movement game and singing activity, then calmed them down with a quiet finger play. "I have a story to tell you," he announced. "Once there were three children, Maria, Josie, and Peng, and they were going camping." Doug continued to tell the story exactly as the children had composed it in their play. Maria, Josie, and Peng smiled and smiled. "That's me!" Peng said.

Doug photocopied the story for each of the three children's portfolios to document their dramatic play and language abilities.

Aline's Story Aline, a teacher of four-year-olds, saw that a child wouldn't eat his potatoes and noted it on his daily report form. She thought, "He's acting out." But as she was filing items in the portfolio, she reviewed her daily report forms and noticed that whenever potatoes were served, this child did not eat them. She realized she was seeing a pattern: "This child just hates potatoes." From then on, when potatoes were served, she offered the child a different food choice.

Teacher Support Possibilities			
Teacher Support	**Non-Mobile Infants**	**Mobile Infants & Toddlers**	**Preschoolers**
Sit beside a child to show your interest. Nod, smile, or simply acknowledge a child's work, saying, "I see."	X	X	X
Describe what the child is doing or playing with to develop vocabulary and oral language.	X	X	X
Respond to the child's vocalizations and actions.	X	X	X
Bring together nonmobile babies.	X		
Provide materials within an infant's reach or just beyond.	X		
Place the baby next to a mirror.	X		
Model the use of a material or toy (such as rolling out playdough, turning a shape box piece until it fits, or taking a turn in a dramatic play role).	X	X	X
Use humor or quiet words to encourage a child to relax while attempting a new activity.	X	X	X
Protect a child's work space by redirecting other children who might jeopardize concentration or hard-earned progress.	X	X	X
Keep up with mobile infants and toddlers to protect them from harm.		X	
Describe what you just saw the child accomplish, even if it's not a completed task.	X	X	X
Invite a child to tell you what she is working on and how she plans to continue.		X	X
Ask children if they want your help.	X	X	X
Anticipate danger and move in as needed.	X	X	X

Louisa's Story Early in the fall, Louisa saved a drawing of a person done by Julio, who was just three years old. Julio had used markers to scribble. There was no recognizable form on the paper. Yet he had told Louisa, "Este soy yo." ("This is me.") She stapled the drawing to a Developmental Milestones Collection Form on which she noted the milestone "Draws shapes and objects in some relation to each other holding marker in fingers instead of fist."

Later in the fall, Julio brought another drawing to Louisa. "Yo dibuje mi mama." ("I drew my mother.") The drawing contained a large circle with two eyes, a nose and mouth, two lines coming out from each side of the circle, and two lines coming out from the bottom (a "potato head" type drawing). Louisa decided to show Julio the other drawing in his portfolio. When he saw the original scribble, Julio said, "¿Yo hice esto?" ("I did that?") "Yo no hice muy bien—era muy pequeño." ("I wasn't very good—I was little.") Louisa invited Julio to see his own portfolio so that she could show him his own progress and celebrate it with him.

Extending Interests

Teachers can use information they gather through observation to extend activities based on children's interests. Going along with children's interests can sometimes prevent behavior problems. Children tend to respond more positively to activities in which they feel that their choices are respected.

Sometimes all that's needed is to acknowledge the child's interest and add related materials to extend that interest. When a child is persistently trying to glue cardboard tubes together without success, a teacher may offer tape so the child can complete the task. When an infant is beginning to look more closely and bat at objects, a teacher may place him in an infant seat under a mobile.

Jodie's Story From her prekindergarten classroom located in an elementary school building, Jodie routinely took children down to the school media center to get books related to topics in which they expressed interest. A child returning from a family trip to the ocean spoke of the sea lions that he had seen and heard. He drew pictures in which the other children expressed interest. Jodie asked the librarian to find resources for the children with pictures and more information about sea lions. The books and video provided much stimulation for children's conversations, projects, further journal writings, and extensions into whales and other sea mammals.

Sometimes a teacher springs off children's interests in a more planned way, organizing a unit of study or project for all of the children in the class. Here's an example of a teacher's curriculum planning based on a child's interest in her new shoes.

Gwen's Story Four-year-old Arianna arrived at the center one day, very excited about having gotten a new pair of running shoes. She enthusiastically told the other children and the teacher about her shopping trip with her mom and her sister. Arianna's teacher, Gwen, wrote down her comments and saved it in her portfolio as a sample of Arianna's descriptive language and communication.

Gwen also picked up on this interest in new shoes as a cue for planning, since she had observed that many children showed excitement when they had acquired new shoes. She decided to set the stage for having the children create a shoe store in the pretend area. She chose this idea because she knew that shopping for shoes is an experience that most of the three- and four-year-olds in her class have in common. She believed that further exploration of this topic would likely be of interest to many, if not all, children in the group.

The shoe store materials included the following:

- shoe boxes filled with different types of shoes, boots, sandals, and slippers
- a shoe measuring device
- a small stool
- shoe polish and laces, a shoe shine brush, and rubber heels
- bags, cash register, and money

By simply providing these materials in the pretend center, she set the stage for shoe store or shoe repair dramatic play to occur.

In addition, Gwen selected books and stories on tape, such as *The Elves and the Shoemaker, The Snowy Day, Cinderella, The Wizard of Oz*—all stories that have shoes as a central or auxiliary theme. Collage or crafts and table activities included foot and hand printing, shoe tracing, lacing frames, and cutting or tearing pictures from shoe company catalogs or shoe store advertising flyers. She planned a walk in the snow for the purpose of making and tracking footprints.

By responding to children's interests in shoes and planning a full unit of study about shoes, Gwen found that there were many different areas of development addressed. Children demonstrated various skills and concepts as they sorted and classified different types of shoes and measured shoe and foot sizes. As they played "shoe store," they demonstrated dramatic play and language abilities. As they tried to tie and buckle, they worked on their fine-motor development. Much of this was then documented for individual portfolios.

Offering Challenge

As you observe children and collect documentation, you are gaining information that can be used to figure out just the right amount of challenge to offer each child in order to further enhance his skills and capabilities.

Some children are not risk takers. They tend to make similar choices of activities over and over again. When you note this on the collection form for Favorites, you may decide that you want to encourage this child to choose a different activity or try something new.

You may have a child who chooses to build with blocks daily, and stays there for long periods of time, but has never visited the writing center in your classroom. You may decide to bring writing materials to this child in the block area, encouraging her to make a sign with her name on it to announce to everyone that she made this construction. You and your colleagues may plan ways to invite this child to participate at the writing center by encouraging her to unwrap new alphabet stampers and pads to be used there. Or you may ask the child to visit the writing center first before going to the block area. All of these curricular decisions challenge the child to take a risk, to try something new, to move out of her comfort zone, so that she can explore different materials that will help develop other skills.

Children who are uncomfortable trying new things often do not respond well to being forced to do so. They may act out, get easily frustrated, or cause problems for other children. Some children will merely obey a teacher's request to do an activity in which the child has no real interest. This is compliance rather than risk taking. Often a child in this situation "gets it over with" as soon as possible. Planning a challenge so that it does not feel forced is essential in preventing the child from simply going through the motions and other unintended behavior problems.

In another example, you may note that a thirteen-month-old is cruising using the furniture in the room, but not yet walking without holding on to your hand or some other support. You know that the next developmental step is walking without support (it's in the Gross-Motor section of the Infant/Toddler Developmental Milestones Chart), so you challenge the child by squatting near him as he stands holding onto a low shelf. You extend your arms and say, "Come to me. You can do it! Come on." You are recognizing the developmental sequence of gross-motor skills and moving the child along that sequence by your interaction with him. You are leading the child's development.

The developmental milestones on which a child is working are at the very edge of the child's capability. Child development theorist Lev Vygotsky calls this "the zone of proximal development." (1995, Berk and Winsler. *See appendix E for reference information.*) By identifying the milestones in this zone (the milestones that are not yet firmly within a child's grasp but that are just barely out of reach), teachers are able to determine exactly what to teach. They are leading development. They are figuring out ways to challenge a child toward new and greater capability, while at the same time offering appropriate support.

We have formatted the developmental milestones in a chart in which related behaviors are grouped together. It allows you to work your way down the list and then across the age groups to see the typical sequence of skill development for each area.

Use these charts to help you plan activities that will lead development and challenge the children. For each child, find the milestone that describes her current level of performance. Then look across the continuum and identify what the next milestone will be. Sometimes just being aware of the next level of complexity for the age range will help you and your teaching colleagues make adjustments in your daily interactions with children. When you incorporate higher expectations that are reasonable, this is another form of developmentally appropriate practice.

For example, if you look at the area of development "Shows interest in others" for infants, you will see a cluster of milestones under birth to eight months of age. These include the following:

- gazing at others
- responding to voices
- smiling and showing excitement when a familiar adult approaches

By reading through this cluster, you get ideas about the types of stimuli to which infants at this age respond. For the same area of development, the slightly older child of eight to eighteen months will be demonstrating a more animated level of interest in others. As you move across the chart, that interest becomes more and more active and complex.

When you read the milestones related to "Shows interest in others," think about how you can expose children to a variety of social situations. Be sure they have increasing opportunities to interact with both adults and peers. Continue to support the development of their expression of feelings toward others.

What you do might look like this:

- putting two babies on the floor near each other with a basket of toys
- at meal times, arranging high chairs such that seated babies are in a semicircle with toddlers, other infants, and adults
- while reading a book, gathering two or three children around you so that the opportunities for interaction are enhanced
- inviting a few older children to the baby/toddler room or outdoor area to create opportunities where mixed age groups come together

To find an example for preschoolers, look at the area of development "Thinking, Reasoning, and Problem Solving." Three-year-olds "actively explore the world around them." They are challenged by and interested in all types of experiences within their home and classroom environments. Looking across the milestones charts, four- and five-year-olds become increasingly interested in the outside world and the larger community.

We know many teachers who routinely weave some aspect of "community" into their classroom plans. Three- and four-year-olds are frequently taken to visit the fire station or the post office. A dentist or a police officer is sometimes invited to visit the classroom and talk about his or her work.

While young children do not understand the composition of a community, these experiences begin to shape a child's concept of "community." In effect, their teachers are exposing these children to information that will eventually be folded into their larger awareness of what a community is and how it functions. Even though the milestone for three-year-olds doesn't make mention of the "interest in the environment beyond home and classroom," the teacher leads development by providing experiences that will challenge children to let in information about the outside world.

The astute teacher of five-year-olds uses classroom life to help explain how communities function. She challenges the children to take into account each other's points of view, rights, and feelings when they make decisions. She may ask children to "take a vote" and abide by the idea of "majority rules." While five-year-olds do not yet understand the concept of "democracy," they are learning to live in community with others. The teacher is exposing them to democratic principles. Once again, these examples illustrate how children are challenged to integrate new information that will eventually lead to a more in-depth concept of community.

You select strategies like those just described because you know what comes next in the developmental sequence for each particular area. You are meeting children on the cusp of their learning, their zone of proximal development. You are providing activities and support to help them develop concepts and interact with the environment and other people.

> Timing Is Everything

Teacher intervention can be helpful, but it can also be intrusive. Interrupting children's play to insert a challenge is not helpful. Observe the scene first. Then stop and consider the type of teacher action that is most suitable. Sometimes, pacing the amount of challenge is critical.

When your goal is to engage children to willingly work on new challenges, you must first provide activities that they already know how to do. Small amounts of challenge can be added to familiar tasks or experiences with which children were previously successful. Children need to encounter nonthreatening situations that allow them to figure out, and then practice, skills that are challenging for them. To achieve this, you sometimes alter the classroom environment by combining new materials with familiar ones, adding to, or moving classroom furnishings. Other times, you decide to provide guidance by asking questions that are meant to help the child move forward in his thinking about a current problem.

> Documenting Children's Responses to Planning

Some children respond to new challenges with enthusiasm. Teachers frequently comment about the joy in seeing "the lightbulb go on" as a child comprehends a new concept or achieves a new skill. By including information in your anecdote about how you changed instructional strategies to help bring about this new understanding or competence, you are documenting additional contextual information to share with family members. Here is an example of an anecdote that describes a child's response to being challenged on the cusp of his development.

"When we place Tyrell (age six months) on the floor in a sitting position, he balances himself and stays seated. If he tries to reach for an object, he topples over and looks toward the object. We sit him back up, and he smiles, and waves his arms, staying balanced for a few minutes."

Some children respond to challenge and new opportunities with wariness and caution. They may make minimal attempts to try new activities. Or they spend time watching others who are involved but do not join in. A child's preference for watching can be significant information for you to document.

Often children are not quite ready for that next step in the developmental sequence. Perhaps muscles aren't developed fully, or more experiences are needed before they can understand a new concept. When a teacher observes a child's caution, and records it in anecdotes, he is signaling himself and his colleagues to pay attention to important information for planning purposes.

The cautious, watching child needs friendly support and encouragement, opportunities to observe others, and, most important, patience and time before progress may be seen. An example follows.

"We have been encouraging Nicholas (age four) to join other children in acting out familiar stories at circle time. (This would help develop his language skills.) For the past week, we have asked him several times if he wants to play a role in the 'Three Little Pigs,' but each day he shakes his head no and buries his face in his hands. When he does this, we tell him that he can watch if that's his choice. He then watches the other children act out the play, and laughs and smiles as they do so.

"Today we asked him if he wanted to be 'the big, bad wolf.' This time, he said, 'Yes,' and stood up with the other children who were the little pigs. He did not say any of the lines out loud, but smiled at the other children and moved to his place beside each of their 'little piggy houses' at the appropriate times in the story."

Finally, some children respond to challenges and higher expectations with absolute avoidance or rejection. These children are communicating that they are not ready to take on the new task or idea. This important signal must be interpreted by teachers as a strong and clear message to "back off" with higher expectations and challenges, at least for a while.

Instead, these children need to practice and refine their skills at the current levels. Providing activities that will guarantee success and increase confidence will be the teachers' planning goals. As they write anecdotes, teachers will document responses to challenging activities, as well as familiar ones. The next example illustrates this point.

"We have been trying to encourage Alicia's fine-motor skills with markers and other writing tools. Alicia (age three) does not choose to write or draw at school. When we invite her to the writing center or the drawing table, she frowns, shakes her head, and says, 'No, I don't want to.' She does use playdough and small manipulative toys such as Legos, stringing beads, and pegboards. We'll concentrate on encouraging her development of fine-motor skills with these materials, and wait a bit longer before we suggest writing and drawing."

To summarize, by becoming a reflective practitioner, stepping back, and thinking about and analyzing every child's typical work and play patterns, you are able to plan more effectively for each child. Using the items collected for the portfolio and the Developmental Milestones Charts to help you, you can appropriately plan the developmental tasks that are best for this child at this time. The cycle of assessment and planning is ongoing. You are continually gathering new information through your observations and selecting the most effective and appropriate teaching strategies.

Your documentation will include an account of how you led and supported the child's development, as well as the child's responses. It will provide a written record to help you track progress (or lack of progress), report to families, and plan even more effectively for each child.

> Ideas for Experienced Users

If you are feeling comfortable with the suggestions offered so far and would like more ideas to apply your observations to your curriculum, read on. If you still need to try things out and gain experience with the Focused Portfolios™ process, you may want to return to this portion of the chapter at a later time.

Writing Multiple Anecdotes That Document Changes in Curriculum

The Tracking Progress with Multiple Anecdotes Form was introduced in chapter 6. By documenting several observations on the form, teachers can record a history of how a child demonstrates accomplishment of a particular milestone. Another way to use this form is to track progress toward the next milestone in the developmental sequence.

On the following pages is an example about Susan, a three-year-old. Her teacher, Marco, first recorded the following details:

- a description of what he saw Susan doing at the water table
- Susan's account of what she was doing
- how much time she spent there
- what she said while playing

Marco noticed that she was moving ahead in her ability to "generate ideas and verbalize her own interpretations of cause and effect," a four-year-old milestone. Therefore, he added materials and asked questions to further challenge Susan to experiment with new concepts and skills. On the Multiple Anecdotes form, he listed the new materials he'd selected, as well as the questions he asked. He tracked Susan's subsequent actions using them and documented her continuing interest in and theories about the properties of water, experimentation with new materials in combination with water, and verbal responses to events and questions.

On the following pages, see Marco's multiple anecdotes about Susan.

Developmental Milestones Collection Form
Version #1 Preschooler

Child's Name Susan Age 3½

Observer Marco Date November 1, 1999

Check off the *areas of development* that apply:

- ☑ Thinking, Reasoning & Problem-Solving
- ☐ Emotional and Social Competency
- ☐ Gross-Motor Development
- ☐ Fine-Motor Development
- ☐ Language and Communication
- ☐ Reading & Writing Development
- ☐ Creative Development

This photo, work sample and/or anecdote illustrates the following *developmental milestone(s):*

Actively explores the world around her; focuses on observable and tangible aspects of objects and events; approaches new tasks and solves problems through observation, trial & error & repetition

Check off whatever applies to the context of this observation:

- ☑ Child-initiated activity
- ☐ Teacher-initiated activity
- ☐ New task for this child
- ☑ Familiar task for this child
- ☑ Done independently
- ☐ Done with adult guidance
- ☐ Done with peer(s)
- ☐ Time spent (1-5 mins.)
- ☑ Time spent (5-15 mins.)
- ☐ Time spent (15+ mins.)

Anecdotal Note: Describe what you saw the child do and/or heard the child say.

Susan chooses the water table almost every day. Today, she pours water on the water wheel again and again. She pointed to it and said to Michael, "Look how it's going around." She poured water from one cup to another, and several times filled a larger cup with several smaller cupfuls. I asked her to tell me what she was doing and she said, "I'm cooking. I have to measure the flour for cookies. One, two, four, five ..."

Tracking Progress through Multiple Anecdotes

Child's Name Susan Area of Development Thinking, reasoning and problem-solving

Anecdotal Note: Describe what you saw the child do and/or heard the child say.

Date: Nov. 19, 1999 Child's age 3½ Observer Marco

Susan asked Marcella to come to the water table with her. "I want to show you how to make the wheel go around." They poured water over the wheel, laughing as it spun. Then they took turns pouring water, with the lever in the open and then in the closed position, bending down to see the results. They agreed that the wheel turned only when the lever was open.

Anecdotal Note: Describe what you saw the child do and/or heard the child say.

Date: Nov. 30, 1999 Child's age 3½ Observer Marco

Susan watched closely as I added snow to the water table. "Where did the snow go? Can I have some?" Scooping up a small ball of snow from the bucket, she dropped it into the water, watching wide-eyed as it melted. "What do you think will happen if we put the snow into a cup without any water?, I asked. She shrugged, took the cup, and added snow. After 7 minutes, she said "It's still white, but there's water in there, too." She spent 25 minutes playing with snow and water today.

Anecdotal Note: Describe what you saw the child do and/or heard the child say.

Date: Dec. 1, 1999 Child's age 3 yrs. 7 mos. Observer Marco

"The snow all melted outside just like in our water table," Susan announced. She explained to her friends yesterday's experiment with snow in the water table and in the cup: "I watched. It didn't melt so fast in the cup." When I asked why she thought the snow outside melted, Susan replied: "Because it was raining in the night." I asked her why she thought the snow melted in the water table. She smiled and said, "Because it's just like the rain."

A series of anecdotes offers teachers comprehensive information within an area of development. It provides well-documented "stories" about

- children's interests
- the way development unfolded toward the next milestone in the sequence
- clear progress made through a series of related events

As you become more experienced, you may choose to write multiple anecdotes to attach to every single Developmental Milestones Collection Form. Or you can be selective and use this tool wherever and whenever it fits.

The Vertical Curriculum

As you respond to children's interests and use them to guide your curricular planning, you will also want to tie your planning and documenting to specific areas of development and milestones within those areas. Planning for activities in the classroom should always be tied closely to children's development. A goal for activity planning is for children and teachers to have fun. Another is to follow the interests of children. Activities can be related to topics that are considered important for young children to learn about (like the seasons or how to be a friend). But, ultimately, having fun does not necessarily lead to learning. Activities must also be related back to the ways that children grow and develop through their experiences. Planning and tracking developmental aspects of each activity help teachers be accountable to their goal of facilitating children's growth and learning.

Earlier in this chapter, we described a teacher's planning related to community and community helpers. Here we take the description of that unit of study one step further and tie it to development. Look at the following chart to see how the teacher referred to specific developmental milestones within several areas of development to guide her planning of a community helpers unit. In the chart, the "horizontal curriculum" refers to the different kinds of activities the teacher planned to meet children's needs in different areas of development. The "vertical curriculum" refers to the way in which the *same* activity (for example, a trip to the fire station or dramatic play in the classroom about the fire station) can meet the needs of children at *different* developmental levels. Note that in the chart, we have only included four sequences of developmental milestones from three areas of development. There are many more milestones that might apply from these same areas of development and from others.

Horizontal and Vertical Curriculum

Areas of Development			
Thinking, Reasoning, and Problem Solving		Emotional Social Competency	Language and Communication
Developmental Milestones			
Five-year-old: Demonstrates interest in exploring aspects of home, school, and community	**Five-year-old:** Uses complex dramatic play often involving many children and planned and scripted through discussion and negotiation of roles	**Five-year-old:** Cooperates in group play and work times most of the time	**Five-year-old:** Participates actively in conversations, listening attentively and with patience to others' contributions
Four-year-old: Explores the immediate environment and some of the environment beyond home or classroom	**Four-year-old:** Uses increasingly complex dramatic play to clarify roles, relationships of self and others	**Four-year-old:** Begins to willingly take turns, mostly to ensure that others will "be friends"	**Four-year-old:** Listens to others and tries to participate in conversation
Three-year-old: Actively explores the world around him or her	**Three-year-old:** Engages in make-believe play and imitates adult roles and responsibilities, and phenomena in their lives	**Three-year-old:** Asserts own needs and wants and is beginning to negotiate conflicts with peers	**Three-year-old:** Begins to listen and attend to others
Classroom Unit of Study: Community Helpers			

Vertical Curriculum ↑

Horizontal Curriculum →

Let's use the example of the study of fire fighters as one way that teachers help children learn about community helpers. Three-year-olds visiting the fire station will enjoy sitting up on the seat of the fire engine, touring the place where fire fighters keep their gear, perhaps trying on a pair of boots or a fire hat. In documenting this field trip, the teacher's notes will likely include references to the three-year-old milestone "actively explores the world around them" or the four-year-old milestone "explores the immediate environment and some of the environment beyond the classroom."

If the group also contains older four-year-olds or five-year-olds, their teacher will likely seek to provide an experience with more depth by asking the fire fighters to talk with the children about such aspects of their work as initial and ongoing training, rotating shifts, and how a 911 call gets dispatched. She may invite the children to prepare their questions in advance of the field trip. She knows that this is a reasonable expectation because it is consistent with the five-year-old milestone "participates actively in conversations, listening attentively and with patience to others' contributions."

Back in the classroom after the field trip, the teacher provides hoses and fire hats, rubber boots and rain coats and observes the children's play to see how they will re-enact and represent their experience. She documents dramatic play, capturing what children say and any vocabulary they use from related stories that may have been read or directly from the field trip. She will likely see a few milestones in the Thinking, Reasoning and Problem Solving Area of Development, including three- and four-year-old milestones such as "engages in make-believe play and imitates adult roles and responsibilities, and phenomena in their lives" or the four- or five-year-old milestones that relate to increasingly complex dramatic play. In the Emotional and Social Competency area of development she's likely to see three- and four-year-old milestones such as "begins to willingly take turns" or "begins to spontaneously offer help, comfort, or objects to others," and five-year-old milestones such as "cooperates most of the time in group play and work time," or "uses language to express feelings, negotiate, and resolve disagreements."

In this unit on community helpers, teachers consult the developmental milestones to guide them in designing experiences that use children's existing skills and also supply new challenges for children at different developmental levels (the vertical curriculum). And these teachers observe children's freely chosen activity to see which milestones each child has accomplished or is working on. In this way, they know which milestones to reference in planning subsequent experiences.

chapter 8

Favorites Collection Form
Child's Name Brandon
Observer Beth
Date October 1998

> Reflecting and Preparing for Family Conferences

Now that you've put together one full collection for each child, how do you share this information with families? How do you find out what families know about their children that you have yet to learn? Family/teacher conferences are a wonderful way to open this discussion. The portfolios you have collected will be the basis for your conversation with families about their children's growth and progress.

We recommend at least two family conferences a year for nine- to ten-month programs, and three for year-round programs. Sample calendars are provided at the end of this chapter.

The focus of your first family/teacher conference of the year is slightly different from the developmental summary that is emphasized at the final conference of the year. This chapter will give the basics for preparing either conference; however, the forms introduced will be for the first conference. Forms and slightly different procedures for preparing the final conference will be discussed in chapter 10.

> Teacher Reflection: Preparing a Conference That's about the Whole Child

During the weeks of portfolio collection, teachers are already engaged in ongoing reflection. As they organize and file photos, work samples, and anecdotes, they are continually looking over the portfolio items and thinking about the best ways to provide and adapt activities to meet children's needs.

A few weeks before family/teacher conferences, reflection of a different kind takes place. It's time now to look over the whole portfolio and put together a full picture of the child's interests and accomplishments, areas of significant progress, and areas to work on further. This reflection will help you determine what to share with the family at conference time and how to further adapt curriculum to meet each child's needs. You will be able to answer the following questions:

- "Over the last few months, what have I learned about this child that I didn't know before?" (interests, accomplishments, progress made, particular areas of challenge or difficulty)
- "How will I best share this information with the family?"
- "How can I best encourage the family to share with me what they think is important about their child and their family?"
- "What input from them will help me set goals and individualize my curriculum for their child?"
- "What teaching strategies worked well and did not work well for this child?"
- "What elements of my total program will change as a result of planning together with each of the families?"

During this reflection process, collection of portfolio items stops. Writing of anecdotes stops. Taking of photographs or collection of work samples stops. This is a time to look back at what you have observed and the items you have collected, an opportunity to think about what you've learned about each child's favorites, friends, family, and developmental milestones.

You will resume the process of observing and documenting, photographing, and collecting after you've met with each child's family in a family/teacher conference. For now, your concern in assessment is a different one. You want to pause to take stock of what you have learned so far.

> The Focused Portfolios™ Reflection and Planning Forms

The Focused Portfolios™ process includes a Reflection and Planning Form to use as you prepare for family conferences. This form helps you organize your thoughts as you look over each child's portfolio. It becomes the official report that summarizes the portfolio collection. You also use the form to conference with family members and formally invite their input and thoughts about their child.

The teacher fills out the first page of the form—Reflection—ahead of time. The second page of the form—Family and Teacher Planning—provides a discussion format. Ideas shared by the teacher and the family members are written down on this page of the form during the conference.

There are two variations of the Reflection and Planning Form that serve as a report on each child at different times in the year. One is used to prepare for one or more conferences that focus on the child's progress up to the end of that collection; the other summarizes the child's overall development for the year. These forms summarize the child's likes, dislikes, interests, habits, and unique characteristics as shown by the information on the Favorites, Friends, and Family forms. In addition, the Reflection and Planning forms show the child's accomplishments, and what the child is currently working on as reflected in the Developmental Milestones forms. Plans for next steps, family member input, and an overall summary are also included.

Copies of these completed reports will be made for the following purposes:

- one to be placed in the child's permanent record
- another to be sent home with families
- a third for your classroom files

The first form, The Focused Portfolios™ Reflection and Planning Form, is designed for continued planning for the child's growth and development. Teachers who are doing two collections during the year use this form only once to summarize the first collection. Teachers doing three collections during the year may use this form for two of their collections.

The second form, The Focused Portfolios™ Reflection and Planning Form: Final Collection, is used to summarize the child's progress and accomplishments for the whole year. Teachers who are doing two collections during the year use this form one time at the end of the year. Teachers who conference three times per year can choose to use this form either before or after the summer collection, or both. Changing forms helps teachers shift their reflection focus at different times of the year.

> What Happens to the Completed Portfolio?

Ultimately, the completed portfolio will be sent home with the family. Most families are delighted to receive the photos and work samples, along with observation notes, as a keepsake of their child's development while attending your program. It is up to the teachers and administrators of each program to determine when to send portfolios home. There are several options.

Most teachers keep the portfolio through at least two collections. They want to see the evidence of a child's progress and stay focused on what to collect the second time around. Keeping the portfolio helps them to follow up on the areas that needed more attention and teacher support for the child. In this instance, the completed portfolio is sent home with the family after the second collection and conference.

Another option is to keep the portfolio until the child is ready to leave the program. By keeping the portfolio for all the years in which the child is in attendance, there is a history of each child's interests and accomplishments to which teachers can refer. The portfolio is also a useful information source for each new teacher as a child moves into different classrooms or as staff turnover occurs.

Some teachers make a copy of the current collection for the family to take home at the time of each conference. They keep the original collection until the child leaves the program. Whichever option is chosen, the family receives a copy of the Reflection and Planning Form after each conference.

> Preparing for Conferences

A few weeks before you are scheduled to conference with family members, make one photocopy of the Reflection and Planning Form for each child. Then take some time to look through each child's portfolio and write down your thoughts.

If you focus reflection on all of the children at the same time, you will find yourself overwhelmed with information, and not able to individualize your thinking to better meet each child's needs. Instead, plan to spend some focused reflection time over the course of a week or two, when, at each sitting, you can think about only two or three children. Perhaps a half hour at the end of each day would work for you, or a block of time in the evening at home. For the month before conferences, you may want to use some of your weekly planning time for reflection. We invite you to figure out the best way to make reflection a priority and to have it work reasonably within your busy schedule. Remember that you are no longer collecting new anecdotes, photos, or work samples. The collection process has stopped so that you can focus on conference preparation.

A copy of the form to be used in the first collection follows on the next pages. *(Forms ready for photocopying can also be found in appendix A.)* On the following pages, step-by-step directions on this reflection process are provided to help you use your time most effectively.

Focused Portfolios™ Reflection and Planning Form

Child's Name ____________________ Age ____ Teacher ____________________ Date ________

Teacher Reflection

Refer to all *areas of development* and to the items in the portfolio

Summarize information from Favorites, Friends, and Family:

List milestones accomplished:

Describe progress that has been observed:

List the milestones that this child is working on (these are the goals for the next collection):

Family and Teacher Planning

Discuss plans to support further development. Write ideas for classroom activities, family involvement, and teacher support. Add any general comments.

Teacher:

Family member(s):

> Steps for Filling Out the Reflection and Planning Form

The "Teacher Reflection" section

1. Look over the Friends, Favorites, and Family Collection Forms for each child. Read your anecdotes and study the photos or work samples. Think about this child's choices, interests, passions, and personality. Think about his family relationships. Ask yourself, "What do these samples tell me about who this child is? What are his characteristics? What personality traits are evident in the way he uses favorite materials, or gets along with others?"

2. Review documentation for each child and identify additional milestone information. Carefully review all the items you have collected. Read through your anecdotes. Look at the photographs. Study the work samples. This documentation should jog your memory of the days when you collected these items. Your recollection will provide even more information and details. As you look through everything collected, including the Friends, Favorites, and Family forms, refer to the Developmental Milestones Charts and identify any milestones that are evidenced in these portfolio items.

Frequently, teachers find that the portfolio items for friends and favorites document children's growing emotional and social competency or blossoming language abilities. Items selected for favorites frequently show some of the milestones that a child has accomplished. The behaviors you see in the categories of friends, favorites, and family may demonstrate milestones from a number of areas of development.

While reviewing the documentation, you may want to write down the milestones you identify in the process. You might choose to add the milestones you've identified directly onto the Friends, Favorites, and Family Collection Forms. Another option is to write them on sticky notes and attach them to the forms.

For example, in her fall collection, Lydia had written the following on the Friends Collection Form for Stephanie: "Stephanie is showing interest in joining groups of children. She saw the other children already seated at the toddler table for snack time. She made eye contact with one of the children, smiled, and then walked to the table. Stephanie reached her hands up to the tabletop and tapped it. I asked her, 'Do you want to sit at the table for snack, Stephanie?' She reached her arms up to me. I sat her down with the others, and again, she smiled at them."

When Lydia read through this anecdote, she realized that the description included several of Stephanie's new developmental skills. She got a sticky note and listed the following from the Developmental Milestones Chart for Infants and Toddlers:

- shows considerable interest in peers
- understands many more words than can say
- walks alone
- sits in chairs unassisted

There's yet another option for adding milestones information. You might prefer to rely on your memory and wait to write it down when you are ready to fill in the Reflection Form. There are teachers who can recall times when they didn't necessarily write an anecdote but witnessed important behavior. Teachers have extensive intuitive knowledge about children based on their recollections of interactions and accomplishments. They use their memory to fill in any gaps. Doing so rounds out the documentation already collected.

3. Based on your documentation and memory, fill out the section called "List milestones accomplished." List the milestones accomplished by the child in each of the areas of development. Take them directly from what you have written on the Developmental Milestones Collection Forms, as well as any milestones you have identified or added to the Friends, Favorites, and Family forms. Review the Developmental Milestones Charts. Select and write any additional milestones observed but still not included. This list of milestones captures what you have seen day in and day out as you interacted with, and observed, each child in your classroom.

When Lydia prepared to fill out the Reflection and Planning Form for Stephanie, she looked over all of the collection forms, photos, work samples, and sticky notes in Stephanie's portfolio and listed the following as milestones accomplished:

- is attentive to adult language
- walks alone
- understands many more words than can say
- sits in chairs unassisted
- creates long babbled sentences
- shows visible reactions to feelings of others
- threads and connects small objects
- actively shows affection for a familiar person
- shows pride, pleasure, and intense feelings for parents

4. Fill in the section "Describe progress that has been observed." Identify ways that this child has shown improvement in skills and greater competency based on your documentation and memory. In this section, you may list milestones from the charts or write descriptions of the child's significant progress in your own words. Because this statement is your evaluation of the child's progress throughout the collection, you can write interpretive statements as you summarize. Here are some examples:

One teacher wanted to celebrate a child's triumph over separation anxiety. Her comment on this progress looked like this:

> *"For the first three weeks, when Jenna came to our classroom, she struggled tearfully when it was time to say good-bye to Mom. Now, she arrives in the morning, greets the teachers, kisses Mom good-bye, and immediately moves into an activity. Jenna's comfort level and sense of security have grown tremendously."*

Here's an example of a teacher's description of an eight-month-old who has persisted in his use of an activity box until he developed the eye-hand coordination to push the buttons and make the sounds.

> *"Daniel's eye-hand coordination with the activity box has improved steadily over the course of four weeks. He is now able to push a button or spin a wheel with his open fingers. We believe that he is aware that the toy will make sounds when he does things to it."*

In writing about Stephanie's progress, Lydia made one summarizing statement and then listed the milestones where she saw significant progress for Stephanie.

> *"Overall, Stephanie has demonstrated that she feels secure and comfortable in the center. She has shown progress in her awareness to make things happen, her exploration of everything around her, interest in other children, and persistence in a task."*

Lydia then planned to discuss Stephanie's progress in more detail with the family members at the conference.

Writing a narrative summary of the progress you have seen (as Jenna's and Daniel's teachers did) and combining that summary with a list of the specific milestones (as Stephanie's teacher did) are two options for completing this section of the Reflection and Planning Form.

5. List the milestones on which the child is currently working. On the milestones charts, locate the behaviors and skills that describe what this child is learning to do now. List these milestones in this section on the Reflection and Planning Form. You may be able to identify one or more milestones for each area of development. For some children, you may not identify any milestones on which they are currently working in some areas of development. That's to be expected.

The behaviors and skills you list in this section will guide your curriculum planning as you begin the next collection. You will combine them with what you have learned about the child's interests, strengths, favorite playmates, family experience, and cultural background. Teachers report that at the end of a portfolio collection, they feel that they really know each child. That depth of knowledge will greatly assist you in setting goals with the family for the next collection period.

For some children, you may earmark one area of development that requires particular emphasis in the coming months. When this is the case, intentionally pinpointing more than one milestone in that area further sharpens the focus of your curriculum planning. Using this strategy, you set the stage for individualizing your work with each child in the next collection period.

The "Family and Teacher Planning" section

6. Think about some strategies you and your colleagues will use in the classroom to support the child's further development. This section is to be completed during the family/teacher conference; however, thinking about and possibly deciding on some classroom strategies ahead of time is appropriate. Here are some suggestions for how to prepare:

Look over what you have written about the milestones and skills on which the child is currently working. Think about any new classroom experiences that can be provided. Consider the various ways that adults can support children's development. Ask yourself the following questions:

- Will the child need close adult support and supervision to accomplish some of these milestones?
- If so, what are the types of adult support we might offer?
- Does this child require time and opportunities to work independently to develop these abilities?
- If so, what will we do to encourage the child toward this goal?
- What classroom activities, materials and/or environmental changes will be introduced to support further development of specific milestones?

Jot down a few notes about how you and your colleagues will support further growth and learning through classroom activities and experiences. These notes can be written on the Reflection and Planning Form before meeting with the family. They will serve as a starting point to the discussion with the family members.

In the following examples, notice the words that are in bold. They are specific actions that the teachers will take to support the child's growth and development.

"Josh (fourteen months old) responds best to Barbara. Barbara ***will model language and interact one-on-one, labeling items*** *played with and* ***asking*** *Josh to repeat words. All staff* ***will urge*** *Josh to walk on his own,* ***providing physical support*** *as needed."*

Here is an example showing a plan to foster independence and persistence:

"Aimee (three years old) does not yet stick with any activities for more than two to three minutes. We'll ***invite*** *her to an activity, and conscientiously* ***stay with her*** *for the first five to ten minutes until she's involved. Before leaving her,* ***we'll encourage her*** *to keep doing what she's doing. We'll* ***check back*** *with her after a few minutes.* ***We will also inquire*** *whether she wants to continue an activity where she left off the day before."*

Here is an example that shows how offering new classroom activities supports the child's development:

"Elijah (four years old)—involved in dramatic play daily with one or two friends. Simple story lines, lots of props, not much planning. ***Will invite*** *Elijah and friends* ***to conference with teacher, and dictate ideas and script*** *to help encourage more complex dramatic play.* ***Discuss ideas*** *for materials, props, set construction, or furniture moving."*

Creating opportunities for family member input is essential. For this reason, leave plenty of space on the form so that you and members of each child's family can share ideas about the best ways to support the child, both in the classroom and at home. You have already written down some of your ideas and now you'll invite them to add their suggestions as well. You can continue to add to the teacher list in response to the family's input.

Save the majority of writing in this section for the last ten minutes of your family/teacher conference. In the next chapter are some suggestions and samples of ways to plan with families. You, the child's family members, and the child will benefit most from an approach that emphasizes your role as partners in helping this child thrive during the period of time you are together.

7. After filling out the Focused Portfolios™ Reflection and Planning Form, take some time to think about what you have written. Now you are ready to step back and reflect on the areas in which you have enjoyed helping this child, and the areas in which you see the child beginning to gain competence. We encourage you to smile and laugh over the fun times the two of you have shared. It's also important to pause and consider the areas about which you might have questions or concerns. Write down these thoughts and anything else that comes to mind that you want to be sure to mention at the conference.

Here is an example of a Reflection and Planning Form that a teacher completed in preparation for the family/teacher conference. Please note that the family section is incomplete pending the results of the discussion at conference time. You may also refer to Sierra's and Linsey's sample collections and the Reflection and Planning Forms in them.

Focused Portfolios™ Reflection and Planning Form

Child's Name Cara Age 5 Teacher Maria Date 12/98

Teacher Reflection
Refer to all *areas of development* and to the items in the portfolio

Summarize information from Favorites, Friends, and Family:

Cara has started to develop some close friendships with Ashley and Janelle. She shows her unique imagination in their pretend play, a favorite for all three of them. Cara often suggests story lines—and tells the other girls about the pretend trips they will take that day. We greatly appreciate your support at school—Cara seems to love it when you volunteer.

List milestones accomplished:

- begins to generate ideas and suggestions, and makes plans and predictions when asked
- uses measurement words (longer, shorter, heavier, lighter)
- participates actively in conversations, listening attentively and with patience to others' contributions
- balances
- rides a bike
- dresses and undresses quickly (self and Barbies and other dolls)
- uses small pegs, beads, and puzzles
- tells a story in sequence
- plays at writing using scribbles and letters
- regularly uses tools (scissors, glue) with control

Describe progress that has been observed:

As Cara grew more comfortable and familiar with the classroom and the other children, she began to gather many children around her and led them in extensive pretend play that included lots of language, imagination, and negotiation. This has become more and more frequent as the fall has gone on. Cara explored more and more expressive art media (paste, collage, paint, drawing).

List the milestones that this child is working on (these are the goals for the next collection):

- counts objects and refers to the quantity of items in talking about them, often demonstrating one-to-one correspondence
- sustains interest in a task, and works hard to solve problems independently or with some adult coaching and support
- uses complex sentence structure and has the vocabulary to express most wants, needs, and explanations without difficulty
- writes using some letters
- uses pencils with growing control

Family and Teacher Planning

Discuss plans to support further development. Write ideas for classroom activities, family involvement, and teacher support. Add any general comments.

Teacher:

To support Cara's writing skills and fine-motor development, we'll provide lots of opportunities for her to explore a variety of uses for pencils, markers and crayons, hole punchers, and scissors. We'll help her with her pencil grasp, and encourage her to write and draw at the Writing Center and Art Area.

We'll continue to encourage Cara to use her excellent language abilities. We'll pay particular attention to coaching her to express herself, especially when conflicts arise.

We'll support Cara in situations where she can lead by suggesting her own ideas and when she can act independently.

Family member(s):

> Sample Calendars for Collections and Conferences

Two sample calendars are provided to show you possible schedules for collections and conferences. The first sample calendar is for programs choosing to do two portfolio collections and conferences per year. The second sample is for those who will collect documentation for three collections and conferences. Please feel free to make any adjustments to suit the needs of your program.

A Two-Collection Schedule

At the end of Collection 1, teachers complete the Reflection and Planning Form as described earlier in this chapter. They focus on future planning to support the child's development of milestones on which she is working. At the end of Collection 2, teachers complete the Reflection and Planning Form: Final Collection. The purpose of this conference is to summarize the child's progress and accomplishments—bringing closure to the child's previous nine months in the program.

For a nine- or ten-month program, Collection 2 will be completed at the end of the program year. Many children will be moving on to another setting. For those who are returning after the summer break, teachers will begin the Focused Portfolios™ process again with a new, first collection relating to the appropriate developmental milestones for the children's age range at that time.

An Informal Fall Meeting You may notice that the first collection period (from September to January) is five months long. Due to the holidays in December, Collection 1 is longer than Collection 2. Recognizing that five months is such a long time, we suggest that you meet with families informally sometime during the fall.

Many programs already schedule a time between late September and early November when families are invited to meet with new teachers and hear about their children's adjustment to classroom routines. These meetings are important times to inform and reassure. If you decide to include these meetings in your fall schedule, and have a few portfolio items to share at that time, by all means, do so. The completed Focused Portfolios™ collections or written Reflection and Planning Forms will not be prepared for these early meetings.

The Sample Calendar for Two Collections a Year follows on the next page.

Sample Calendar for Two Collections a Year	
Collection 1: September – January	**Collection 2: February – May**
September–early December Ongoing collection of portfolio items: • writing anecdotes • taking photographs • collecting work samples in the classroom	**February–early April** Ongoing collection of portfolio items: • writing anecdotes • taking photographs • collecting work samples in the classroom
Mid- to late December Complete the collection: • Favorites, Friends, and Family (one form for each) • Developmental Milestones Collection Forms (minimum seven)	**Mid- to late April** Complete the collection: • Favorites, Friends, and Family (one form for each) • Developmental Milestones Collection Forms (minimum seven)
January Collection stops for the month: • Weeks 1 & 2: Teacher Reflection (Prepare the Reflection and Planning Forms) • Weeks 3 & 4: Family/Teacher Conferences	**May** Collection stops for the month: • Weeks 1 & 2: Teacher Reflection (Prepare Reflection and Planning Forms—Final Collection) • Weeks 3 & 4: Family/Teacher Conferences

An informal meeting with families in late September to early November may be scheduled. No written reports are required. Sharing portfolio items is optional.

A Three-Collection Schedule

The schedule for Collection 1 and Collection 2 will probably look the same whether your program is doing two or three collections per year. When doing three collections per year, at the end of Collection 1 teachers complete the Reflection and Planning Form as described earlier in this chapter. They focus on future planning to support the child's development of milestones on which he is working.

For twelve-month programs, the completion of Collection 2 will not necessarily occur at the end of the child's year in the program. Year-round programs need flexibility in using the Focused Portfolios™ process. In our design, we assumed that when a teacher works with a child for a period of nine months, she wants to summarize the child's progress and accomplishments at the end of that time frame. Therefore, our sample calendar recommends using the Final Collection Form after the second collection. You and your colleagues will need to make programmatic decisions regarding your own scheduling of conferences and use of the appropriate Reflection and Planning Forms.

For many year-round programs, the summer months are a more relaxed time, when expectations for curriculum and portfolio documentation may be somewhat less than during the rest of the year. Many teachers and families take vacations during the summer months. This is likely to interrupt ongoing assessment in the classroom. Nonetheless, as more of the planned activities shift to the outdoors and to special field trips, there will be numerous opportunities for portfolio documentation.

Therefore, the sample calendar includes a shorter time period with several adaptations for summer collection and conferencing. Summer teachers will complete as much of the portfolio as they can. As a program, you can choose which of the two versions of the Reflection and Planning Forms to use in August. The deciding factor would be whether teachers will include future planning or summarize only the child's summer accomplishments. An informal set of family/teacher conferences can be held at the end of the summer session. Decisions regarding conferences are left to the discretion of each program.

Sample Calendar for Three Collections a Year

Collection 1: September –January	Collection 2: February–May	Collection 3: June–August
September–early December Ongoing collection of portfolio items: • writing anecdotes • taking photographs • collecting work samples in the classroom	**February–early April** Ongoing collection of portfolio items: • writing anecdotes • taking photographs • collecting work samples in the classroom	**June–mid-July** Ongoing collection of portfolio items: • writing anecdotes • taking photographs • collecting work samples in the classroom
Mid- to late December Complete the collection: • Favorites, Friends, and Family (one form for each) • Developmental Milestones Collection Forms (minimum seven)	**Mid- to late April** Complete the collection: • Favorites, Friends, and Family (one form for each) • Developmental Milestones Collection Forms (minimum seven)	**Mid- to late July** Complete as much of the collection as you can: • Favorites, Friends, and Family • Developmental Milestones Collection Forms
January Collection stops for the month: • Weeks 1 & 2: Teacher Reflection (Prepare the Reflection and Planning Forms) • Weeks 3 & 4: Family/Teacher Conferences	**May** Collection stops for the month: • Weeks 1 & 2: Teacher Reflection (Prepare Reflection and Planning Forms—Final Collection) • Weeks 3 & 4: Family/Teacher Conferences	**August** Collection stops for the month: • Weeks 1 & 2: Teacher Reflection (Prepare the Reflection and Planning Forms of your choice) • Weeks 3 & 4: Informal Family/Teacher Conferences

The summer months provide countless new documentation opportunities with the abundance and variety of outdoor experiences.

Integrating New Children into the Assessment Cycle

Some children may begin attending a program in the middle or near the end of a collection period. When this occurs, you may choose to wait until the end of the next collection period before writing Reflection and Planning Forms and scheduling family/teacher conferences. Interim meetings with these families can be scheduled to provide information about how their children are settling in and to answer any questions about the program. If you have portfolio items that you wish to share at that time, by all means do so.

Quarterly Reports for Young Children with Special Needs

Programs serving young children with special needs using this assessment tool are finding that the process outlined in this book (with two collections and conferences) is adaptable to the quarterly report requirements. Teachers collect documentation and report quarterly on what they have gathered up to that point. The goal is to schedule a family/teacher conference to review the complete portfolio at the end of the second quarter and again at the end of the fourth. In these programs, many of the portfolio items are directly tied to Individual Family Service Plan or Individual Education Plan goals, so that the documentation becomes a tool for demonstrating progress toward these goals.

chapter 9

Favorites Collection Form
Child's Name Brandon
Observer Beth
Date October 1998

> Effective Conferencing with Families in the First Collection

You have carefully reviewed your first collection, thought deeply about each child's accomplishments and future goals, and filled out the Reflection and Planning Form. Now you are ready to meet with family members who are eager for information about their children.

In this chapter, we offer a variety of suggestions to help make conferences appropriate for families. These suggestions are by no means all-inclusive. You and your colleagues will need to consider your own situation as you plan to meet with family members to share portfolios.

> Setting the Tone for a Conference

Our job as teachers is to set a warm, friendly, and respectful tone for conferencing. Teachers and family members are on the same team—one that is rooting for the same child. All have the same goal in mind—the most successful learning experience for this little one. Emphasizing that partnership is one important way to set a welcoming tone.

As you think about the conference process, it is essential to look closely at the different cultures represented by the families in your program. Meeting with family members to discuss their children is a potentially sensitive business. For some families, teachers represent power. In other instances, family members feel as if the teacher in the conference setting is judging them. The teacher's job of creating an effective conference means respecting feelings, emphasizing an equal partnership, and honoring culturally varied communication styles.

Some adults feel intimidated by teachers. For them, perhaps it is the teacher's tone that is off-putting. For others, their own experiences with schooling may not have been positive ones, and those recollections bring forth uncomfortable feelings. Cultural differences in communication styles or social/economic class issues can come into play. Sometimes adults may not have fully established a sense of confidence in the parenting role. These family members question themselves and fear that teachers are judging their abilities to raise a child effectively.

Educating yourself about the cultural backgrounds of the families in your program is an ongoing job and has particular importance at conference time. In a town in Northern California where many Thai and Cambodian refugees have settled, teachers met with the leaders of the Southeast Asian community to learn more about expectations, cultural traditions, and approaches. In the family/teacher conferences, one of these community leaders often attended with the family. He served not only as an interpreter but also as an important member of the larger family who cared deeply about each child in its community.

We have deliberately used the word *families* and not *parents* in talking about conferences to acknowledge that children live in many different family structures. It's important that families decide who should attend the conference, and we encourage any adult in the family who spends a lot of time with the child or has a significant part in raising the child to attend. It's also important that all family members who attend the conference feel welcome. This may mean welcoming grandparents, adult siblings, and aunts and uncles into the discussion. Perhaps a community leader will attend, as in the example above; it may mean that one parent, or two, or four (in the case where a child has stepparents) attend. Perhaps two conferences have to be scheduled with two sets of parents who are sharing custody, or perhaps a child has two moms or two dads. Whatever the child's family structure, it is the teacher's job to make sure the conference is welcoming to that child's family.

Informal Conferencing

For some teachers, the conference process is informal and ongoing. For example, in a small town in New Mexico, teachers frequently meet children and their families in the bank or the grocery store. And in the process of saying "Hello" and exchanging pleasantries, family members often ask, "How is he doing at school?" The teachers have found that it helps build positive relationships with the families if they respond by recounting a recent incident (one they very well may have documented for the portfolio). They always make sure that the story told has a positive tone, realizing that they are in a public place and that confidentiality may be an issue. Family members may share a story from home as well. There are smiles and warm feelings all around in these "mini-conferences."

In her teen parenting program in Illinois, Sharon Mann found that conferencing was almost a daily process. As the fourteen- through seventeen-year-old moms and dads dropped off and picked up their children, Sharon shared with them the portfolio documentation she did that day—either showing them the photos she and her colleagues took, or telling them anecdotes about things their children did. She continually helped these young parents learn about appropriate expectations for their children and ways to support healthy growth and development. She also made a point of asking these parents to share their stories and responded fully to any questions or concerns they had.

Even in these programs that use an ongoing conferencing approach, it is still recommended that a formal portfolio review be scheduled. This gives you and the family members an opportunity to share all of the information about the child in a more comprehensive way.

Inviting Family Members to Conferences

Announcing the purpose and schedule of upcoming conferences is an important task. You want to explain why family involvement at conferences ultimately benefits the child, the family, and the teacher. If family members speak a language other than that spoken in the center, any written communication sent home should be in the native language of the family, and it's important to be sure that at least one adult member of the family can read. At the West Chicago Early Childhood Bilingual Programs, teachers write all family newsletters and announcements in Spanish, the first language of the children in attendance. In addition, all of their documentation in the portfolio, as well as the Reflection and Planning Forms, are written in Spanish.

At Centre de la Petite Enfance Tchou-Tchou in Montréal, forms, family letters, and portfolios are completed in either French or English, depending on the family's first language. *(Collection forms that have been translated into Spanish are included in appendix B.)*

You want families to know that you hope for 100 percent participation and that you will make accommodations to achieve this goal. At the Indiana School for the Deaf, American Sign Language interpreters are provided at conference time for any family member who needs them. If wheelchair accessibility is an issue, plan to have the conference in a location that is accessible. These accommodations, and others needed by people with disabilities, are required by the Americans with Disabilities Act.

Notifying families ahead of time of these arrangements helps overcome some of the concerns they may have about the family/teacher conference. Plan to communicate with families about the conferences several times:

- first, in the registration materials they receive
- then in the regular newsletters and communications you send them
- and finally in special announcements or phone calls as the dates approach

In Orcas Island, Washington, Martha Inch sends a letter similar to the following to tell her families about the portfolio system that she is using as an assessment tool.

Dear Parents,

Our staff uses a process of documentation called "Focused Portfolios™" to record children's growth and development. Through photographs, anecdotes, and children's work samples, teachers put together a visual account of each child's accomplishments. Using recognized developmental milestones, growth in the following seven areas of development is assessed:

1. Thinking, Reasoning, and Problem Solving
2. Emotional and Social Competency
3. Language and Communication
4. Gross-Motor Development
5. Fine-Motor Development
6. Reading and Writing Development
7. Creative Development

The Focused Portfolios™ process recognizes and celebrates that all children develop at different rates and with various strengths. Collections are completed in fall and spring and kept in a folder as long as the child is enrolled in the program. At the end of the child's enrollment, the portfolio becomes a memento to be taken home and treasured.

This collection is a representation of the child as an individual with distinct interests, background, skills, and desires. We will meet with you in family/teacher conferences twice a year to share these treasured collections and celebrate the accomplishments of your child.

Some programs find that home visits for conferencing may be an effective strategy with some families. Programs that already include home visiting as a part of their services often weave the conference into their already scheduled visits, instead of setting up a separate time to go over the portfolio. Calling families to explain your goals and options for setting up the conferences may be a helpful step.

Extending an invitation that is welcoming, warm, and friendly is essential. You want to make the process of conferencing sound pleasant and informative, as opposed to intimidating or judgmental. We suggest that telling family members exactly what to expect may be helpful. Assuring them that you will not be talking "at" them but rather "with" them will emphasize the conversational nature and the intent of the conference. Suggest that prior to coming to the conference, they might like to think about any questions and concerns they have that can assist them in organizing and preparing their thoughts, or things they want to make sure you know about their children. Some teachers send home a letter outlining the process and including a few questions to consider. This step may facilitate advance-written preparation by family members. For family members who are unable to read or write, a phone call or home visit can be arranged so that the same information can be passed along.

Accommodating Family Schedules

Schedule conferences at family members' convenience. Offer early-morning, late-afternoon, or evening conferences. Some family members can only attend during a lunch hour. Again, conferencing in the family's home may be more convenient. Scheduling over a two-week period may help to accommodate the different needs of families.

A commitment to effective conferencing necessitates administrative decisions regarding how best to accommodate family schedules and differences in communication style. This commitment signals quality in an early childhood program. Achieving 100 percent family participation will necessitate some flexibility and careful planning, and it should be every program's goal.

One way to support family involvement is to provide child care during the actual conference for the child in the program, as well as for any siblings who might need it. Then family members can fully engage with the teacher and not be distracted by the needs of their children. A "play room" can be set up with quiet manipulatives, playdough, books, and a light snack. Staff members can be rotated to supervise these children. It may be necessary to remind parents that these special child care arrangements are offered only for as long as family members are meeting with teachers.

If it is not possible to have a separate space or staff coverage for children and siblings, then inviting them to be present at the conference is another option. We suggest that you have those same quiet activities available. If you work with older toddlers or preschoolers, encourage the child in your program to be a part of the conference when the portfolio is reviewed. She may be able tell stories in her own words about the photographs or work samples included. He may have a favorite work sample or photo that he wants to talk about. Invite the child to participate during the first part of your conference. Then offer the child quiet activities or a light snack, while you and the family members talk in more detail and decide on goals and plans to support the child's further development.

Please do not consider turning away families who cannot attend because they have no one to stay with their children. Remember that the goal is 100 percent participation. Conferencing is too important for both teacher and family members for anyone to be excluded. Using flexible and supportive approaches will guarantee the best possible response from families. And, once the family members see the portfolios, they will likely agree that it was worth the effort to be a part of this important meeting.

Another option is to conference with families in their homes. Arranging a time that is convenient for the family, taking the portfolio to them, and sharing all you know about their child can be extremely valuable. The opportunity to observe the child in her home environment provides additional perspective and helps the teacher know the child better after this experience. In addition, the family often enjoys welcoming the teacher. And usually older toddlers or preschoolers are thrilled to see their beloved teacher outside of the school or center setting.

We do not recommend telephone conferencing. This format is not an effective option for discussing a portfolio. The face-to-face meeting between teachers and family members provides an opportunity to strengthen communication on behalf of the child. However, when no other option is workable, a telephone conference may have to be arranged. First, you will need to make a photocopy of all the portfolio items. Before the phone conversation, send the copies home for the family members to review. Then you can refer to specific portfolio items in your discussion. The same conference format as outlined in this chapter can be followed.

We have presented a range of options to accommodate families that may necessitate some shifts in staff schedules. Administrators want to make certain that teachers are given enough preparation time and opportunities to reflect carefully about individual children. A longer conference schedule must recognize and respect any extra time that teachers are being asked to be away from their own families.

Teacher safety and compensation for work done outside of normal schedules need to be addressed.

- Will compensation take the form of time off or additional pay?
- Depending on the security of a neighborhood or the time of day, is it safest to send teachers out in pairs (lead teacher and assistant) rather than alone?

When conferences are all bunched together in one or even two to three days, teachers generally feel overwhelmed and are unable to engage as authentically or thoughtfully as they would like. To allow ample time for reflection and conferencing, many programs devote a full month in their schedule to this process: two weeks for reflection and two weeks for conferencing.

A Pleasant Conference Environment

Thinking about the family members' comfort is another way to set a positive and welcoming tone. Using adult-sized chairs (and comfortable ones if at all possible) is much preferred to using child-sized seating. Setting the chairs around a clutter-free table or desk is important so that the portfolio can easily be reviewed. Placing a vase with flowers on a nearby table along with coffee or lemonade and cookies is another way of saying, "I'm glad you're here."

Being clear about the time frame and agenda of the conference is a way to put people at ease. You can send home a published agenda along with your newsletter confirming conference appointment times. A possible division of time might be

- ten minutes for the family to raise their issues and concerns
- about ten to twenty minutes for review of the portfolio and Reflection page
- ten minutes to jointly set goals and plans for the child

Clarifying the time frame allows you to assume the role of timekeeper and helps you to politely move the conversation along. Restating the time available at the outset of the conference serves as a useful reminder. If you do not let family members know what to expect you may be viewed as interrupting, rude, or intimidating, rather than helpful, polite, and mindful of the time.

> How Long Should an Effective Conference Be?

We recommend that thirty to forty-five minutes be scheduled to allow enough time to review the items in the portfolio and to engage families in a meaningful discussion about what the child has accomplished and what next steps to plan. An effective family conference that includes a portfolio to review requires more time than has been traditionally scheduled. Most teachers express frustration that the typical twenty minutes allotted for conferences is not enough time to adequately talk about the child and refer to portfolio items.

Some teachers invite members of the child's family to arrive ten to fifteen minutes prior to the scheduled conference time. During that time, family members can review their child's portfolio without the teacher being present. If conferencing in a home-visit situation, teachers may send the portfolio home for the family members to review before the scheduled visit. This allows families time to enjoy the portfolios on their own in a more leisurely way. It also helps preserve the face-to-face meeting time for in-depth discussion and sharing.

In a thirty- to forty-five-minute meeting, the teacher and family members can

- exchange their responses to the portfolios
- ask and answer questions
- hear each other's comments
- set goals and make plans together

The teachers who have tried this format report positive family feedback and excellent results. Specific comments from teachers in the Peoria, Illinois, pilot project included the following.

"Parents loved the pictures."

"Families made comments like, 'I didn't realize you did all this and worked on all these areas.'"

"They particularly liked anecdotal comments and photos. My conferences had much more discussion and parent participation. It sparked ideas for parents and they told me more about their child at home."

"I found it so much easier to talk objectively about a child who had problems. The family members could see it right there in black and white. They didn't think it was just my opinion."

Some teachers give families the choice of including their preschoolers in the portfolio review time. In this way, the child has the opportunity to talk about what appears in the photographs and add a personal point of view to the written anecdotes. Whichever approach is selected, there needs to be plenty of time for teacher and family members to review the portfolio together and converse in an unhurried and pleasant way.

> What to Say and How to Say It

Inviting family members to talk and share first is a very powerful way of valuing their contribution. Asking some specific questions and welcoming their responses will help them relax and feel more comfortable. Such questions might include

- "What does your child like about our program?"
- "Is there any information you would like me to know about your child?"
- "Do you have specific concerns about your child's growth and development or progress at school?"
- "What do you hope we'll accomplish today?"

Questions like those above can be on the conference preparation form for families that we mentioned earlier in the chapter.

Your tone of voice and attitude are the most critical elements to consider when planning and implementing an effective family conference. Again, awareness of cultural differences is essential. In some cultures, direct eye contact is not considered respectful. Learning more about how to communicate appropriately in various cultures while still focusing on the mutual interest in the child is an important part of each teacher's role.

In early childhood education programs, teachers are asked to adopt an unbiased demeanor when meeting with families. To be professional, they must express an open, friendly, and supportive attitude. Even if family members express dissatisfaction with certain methods, teachers must be willing to acknowledge, learn, and hear what the family has to say, and to consider their feedback carefully. If a teacher has any concerns about a child, or has a history of conflict with a family, professional behavior must include willingness to honestly assess bias. The goal is to find common ground for open, ongoing dialogue. That's not always an easy task, but certainly it is an essential one.

Behaviors That Promote or Inhibit Communication

In the following tables, behaviors are listed that can promote or inhibit communication. It may not apply to all cultural groups, but it gives teachers suggestions for consideration. Read through the lists and think about the families in your program.

Inappropriate Teacher Communication	Appropriate Teacher Communication
• Telling, not listening • Calling family members by first name (but expecting to be addressed as "Mrs.") • Acting like you don't care about their child and family • Looking at clock/watch; rushing the discussion • Avoiding eye contact (in some cultures) • Using "teacher language" or hiding information • Being rigid • Acting inconsistently • Blaming • Touching (for some cultures)	• Speaking with respect and listening carefully • Asking how to address the family members, and letting them know what to call you • Demonstrating that you care about their child and family • Allowing enough time for all questions to be answered • Making eye contact (for some cultures) • Using friendly humor (for some) • Giving explanations in simple, straightforward language • Providing options and flexibility • Following through • Being accountable • Touching (for some cultures)

> Reviewing the Portfolio with Family Members

The next step is to review the portfolio with the family members. You will probably talk about much more than you have written on the forms in the portfolio. Feel free to do so. You are a storyteller—and the focus of your stories is the child. You can add more details as you look at the portfolio samples, fill in more about the context of the child's experiences, and describe and enjoy the accomplishments of each child.

If families have had a chance to look at the portfolio in advance, invite and welcome their stories and reactions. Ask if they have any comments or questions, or if there was anything in the portfolio that they want to know more about.

If a family has not reviewed the portfolio yet, the next step is to do so with them. You can use the Reflection and Planning Form, which you have partially completed, to guide your discussion. As you go through the collection together, be sure to allow opportunities for family members to comment and question. The conference is meant to be a "give and take" conversation, not a one-sided "lecture" on your part.

By beginning your review of the portfolio with the Favorites, Friends, and Family pieces, you start on a positive note. This is a chance to celebrate the child's uniqueness, his interests, frequent choices, and special friends. Children's likes and dislikes (what they tend not to choose) are often evident in these portfolio items. It's also an opportunity to recognize the importance of family in the child's life by asking family members to tell some stories about the child at home. Teachers report that family members respond warmly to this portion of the portfolio—it often corroborates what they already know about their child. Listen to the family's comments and take notes about the child's interests or personality characteristics that are different than those known to you. In this way, the conference becomes a mutual sharing process where both you and the family members are learning new things about who the child is.

Next, discuss the milestones that the child has accomplished and show the relevant portfolio samples. This continues the positive focus set early in the conference. As you offer more information to accompany each of the photos or work samples, you are sharing what you have seen the child do and heard the child say. You are identifying the child's strengths, skills, competencies, and behaviors that are seen frequently. Again, you can ask the family members if this seems true in their experience of their child—or do they have a different perspective? Is the child showing the same or different strengths and competencies at home?

You can decide how much of the actual language of the Developmental Milestones Charts you wish to use. In some instances, you may wish to use more conversational terms to describe a child's development. In the Shima Yazhi home-visiting program in New Mexico, parents have told the teachers: "Don't show me some piece of paper—tell me what my child is doing and what it means." Respecting this request, teachers spend more time with the actual portfolio pieces, using language that describes exactly what children are doing rather than listing the milestone information.

Next, referring to actual portfolio samples, identify areas where you have seen progress. You may read your comments from the form or casually converse about interpretation and evaluation of the child's accomplishments. Invite family members to ask questions and make comments as you go along. Celebrate with them the important developmental steps their child has taken.

As you proceed to sharing developmental milestones on which the child is working, you may not have actual portfolio samples that document these milestones. Instead, explain to the family what you are seeing in the classroom that tells you that the child is currently learning something new. Ask them if they see their child attempting anything new at home but not quite getting it yet. Find out if there are things that they don't see their child doing yet but that they wonder about. Communicate to them that these emerging skills, behaviors, and milestones that you are discussing will be the new focus for classroom planning in the coming months.

If you have any concerns about the child's development, this is the point in the conversation to raise them. Once again, invite families to express any concerns that they may have. Provide reassurance that identifying these concerns helps you focus and individualize planning and that these issues will be addressed in natural and nonthreatening ways. Let family members see your positive approach to supporting the child's development.

This leads you directly into discussion of the second page of the Reflection and Planning Form, where teacher and family members plan strategies to support the child in the classroom and at home. If you have already identified some classroom strategies that you and your colleagues will be using with this child, share those now.

Invite the family members' questions and comments. What would they like to see happen for their child? Are there things they want teachers to do in the classroom that they see as important for their child? Can they do some things at home to support the classroom efforts? The discussion can proceed with shared goals, ideas, and plans for both school and home, as well as a plan for ongoing communication about the child's progress.

Teachers have found that inviting families to share their thoughts in writing delights and sometimes surprises family members. However, families may hesitate to follow through. Family members may want to attend the conference, see the portfolio, and hear what the teacher has to say. Then, after reflection, they may be prepared to put their own comments on paper. If only one parent attends the conference, he or she may wish to discuss and compose a response with his or her spouse. Two teachers in West Chicago considered these factors in crafting strategies to help families in this regard.

Knowing that she wanted families to contribute to the Reflection and Planning Form at the conference, Veronica Cisowski sent families a brief letter with information about conference dates and times. Included in her letter were four questions that she asked them to consider and come prepared to talk about at the family/teacher conference:

1. Do you have any worries or concerns about your child?
2. Is there any exciting or interesting news at your house?
3. Is there anything specific you want to know about your child at school?
4. What are some of your family's hobbies or special interests?

Veronica reported that 100 percent of her families came prepared to discuss these questions (many with their comments written out). She saw this two-way discussion as a springboard for jointly setting goals in family/teacher planning.

Pam Giermann invited family members to take the Reflection and Planning Form home and return it after they had added their written comments. She suggested that they write about any of the following topics:

- their reaction to the portfolio, Reflection and Planning Form, and the conference in general
- their goals, wishes, and dreams for their child in the program
- their questions or concerns after reviewing the portfolio and conferencing with the teacher
- any additional information they might want to share about their child

Pam received a written response from every one of the families with whom she had conferenced. She said she learned a great deal more about each of the children and was often moved by the supportive comments she received regarding her teaching. She was struck by the heartfelt commitment family members expressed to further helping their children.

> Ending the Conference

At the end of the conference, express your appreciation to families for their involvement and thank them for their willingness to work with you in a home/school collaboration. On the Reflection and Planning Form, write down all of your mutually agreed-upon ideas. Explain how this will guide you in working toward the next collection for the portfolio. Tell them that when you all meet again, either at the next family/teacher conference or during casual, daily interactions, you can update each other on the progress the child is making toward the goals you jointly set. Give the family a copy of the completed Reflection and Planning Form. If you cannot easily photocopy right in the conference setting, tell them when they can expect a copy. Follow through as soon as you possibly can.

Involving the family, listening carefully to their ideas, validating their concerns, and reassuring them of your commitment to the partnership for the sake of their son or daughter are indicators of quality in early childhood education. Generously sharing the portfolio in a conference and including families in setting goals are also characteristics of high-quality practice.

The following list summarizes the key points we have made about an effective family/teacher conference.

A Summary of an Effective Family/Teacher Conference

- Take responsibility for learning about the cultural priorities and needs of the families represented by the children in your program and be prepared to honor them.
- Welcome family members; invite them to get some coffee or lemonade and make themselves comfortable. Be sensitive to cultural norms and different ways of communicating.
- Spend a few minutes on introductions and personal conversation—make reference to the child's positive comments about one or more of the members present, or something special that happened recently (e.g., "I understand Grandma just visited from St. Louis").
- Ask family members if they have any questions they might like to ask.
- Reiterate the time frame and format for the conference.
- Invite family members to talk first and share some of their thoughts about their child's growth and development, as well as any concerns or questions they may have.
- The Reflection and Planning Form is your conference agenda. Use it to go through the portfolio items. Again, continually invite family member input. This is a conversation, a give and take, with both of you learning more about the child.
- Together with the family members, plan strategies to support the child's ongoing development in the classroom and at home.
- Give (or send) family members a copy of the completed Reflection and Planning Form. Let them know they will receive the completed portfolio at the end of the program year.
- Thank family members for coming. Let them know how to reach you for ongoing communication.

On the following pages are completed Reflection and Planning Forms for two children: Cara, a preschooler (whose Reflection and Planning Form appeared in chapter 8), and Matthew, a toddler. They include input from family members about supporting the children's development, and the goals they have identified for their respective children. You may also wish to look at Sierra's and Linsey's Reflection and Planning Forms in the sample collections (in chapters 3 and 6). There you can see how their parents responded in conferences.

Focused Portfolios™ Reflection and Planning Form

Child's Name Cara Age 5 Teacher Maria Date 12/98

Teacher Reflection

Refer to all *areas of development* and to the items in the portfolio

Summarize information from Favorites, Friends, and Family:

Cara has started to develop some close friendships with Ashley and Janelle. She shows her unique imagination in their pretend play, a favorite for all three of them. Cara often suggests story lines—and tells the other girls about the pretend trips they will take that day. We greatly appreciate your support at school—Cara seems to love it when you volunteer.

List milestones accomplished:

- begins to generate ideas and suggestions, and makes plans and predictions when asked
- uses measurement words (longer, shorter, heavier, lighter)
- participates actively in conversations, listening attentively and with patience to others' contributions
- balances
- rides a bike
- dresses and undresses quickly (self and Barbies and other dolls)
- uses small pegs, beads, and puzzles
- tells a story in sequence
- plays at writing using scribbles and letters
- regularly uses tools (scissors, glue) with control

Describe progress that has been observed:

As Cara grew more comfortable and familiar with the classroom and the other children, she began to gather many children around her and led them in extensive pretend play that included lots of language, imagination, and negotiation. This has become more and more frequent as the fall has gone on. Cara explored more and more expressive art media (paste, collage, paint, drawing).

List the milestones that this child is working on (these are the goals for the next collection):

- counts objects and refers to the quantity of items in talking about them, often demonstrating one-to-one correspondence
- sustains interest in a task, and works hard to solve problems independently or with some adult coaching and support
- uses complex sentence structure and has the vocabulary to express most wants, needs, and explanations without difficulty
- writes using some letters
- uses pencils with growing control

Family and Teacher Planning

Discuss plans to support further development. Write ideas for classroom activities, family involvement, and teacher support. Add any general comments.

Teacher:

To support Cara's writing skills and fine-motor development, we'll provide lots of opportunities for her to explore a variety of uses for pencils, markers and crayons, hole punchers, and scissors. We'll help her with her pencil grasp, and encourage her to write and draw at the Writing Center and Art Area.

We'll continue to encourage Cara to use her excellent language abilities. We'll pay particular attention to coaching her to express herself, especially when conflicts arise.

We'll support Cara in situations where she can lead by suggesting her own ideas and when she can act independently.

Family member(s):

Cara's mom and dad agreed that Cara could use more help and support in the ways she grasped a pencil and attempted to write her name and make letter-like shapes. They decided that they would put together a special "Writing Box" for Cara to keep in the family kitchen. This box would contain several different kinds of paper, writing tools, and letter stencils.

Mom and Dad will encourage Cara to get out her "Writing Box" while dinner is being cooked, or when her mom is writing a grocery list. Cara's parents said that they wanted their home environment to contribute to her growth in writing and fine-motor skills as well.

While discussing fine-motor skills, we all agreed it would be helpful to offer playdough and clay for Cara to strengthen the small muscles of her hands and fingers. We talked about the importance of presenting all of the above activities in a pleasant, non-forced way.

Focused Portfolios™ Reflection and Planning Form

Child's Name Matthew Age 2 years Teacher Sara Date Jan. 1999

Teacher Reflection

Refer to all *areas of development* and to the items in the portfolio

Summarize information from Favorites, Friends, and Family:

Matthew's personality is really showing in his love of costumes and pretend play. He plays alongside other children, especially Pierre and Brianna. Thanks for sending in the photos of your trip to Disney World. Matthew points to the pictures and tries to name the characters.

List milestones accomplished:

- explores objects through touch
- labels objects using new vocabulary
- enjoys playing near and with other children
- understands many more words than can say
- puts on garments (cap)
- engages in make-believe play and imitates adult roles
- explores the uses and properties of expressive media
- combines words in two- and three-word sentences
- plays pretend games
- listens to short stories
- picks up smaller objects easily
- uses a variety of manipulative toys
- shows strong sense of self as individual evidenced by "me" and "mine"
- demonstrates interest in what others are doing
- actively shows affection for familiar person
- displays feelings mostly through behavior rather than words

Describe progress that has been observed:

- beginning to express feelings with words some of the time
- responding more and more to conversations and questions
- concentration and time spent on tasks is increasing (listening to stories, playdough, music)
- vocabulary increasing—self-expression—needs and wants

List the milestones that this child is working on (these are the goals for the next collection):

- uses words and simple phrases to express some feelings (words instead of hitting)
- verbalizes awareness of feelings of others
- learning words to simple finger plays, songs, etc.
- attempts to use various tools to express self though random marks, painting
- engages in pretend play

Family and Teacher Planning

Discuss plans to support further development. Write ideas for classroom activities, family involvement, and teacher support. Add any general comments.

Teacher:

- teach and encourage self-help skills (dressing self)
- exposure to a wider variety of fine-motor skill activities, with encouragement
- model additional ways to be assertive with peers, using more words; model and coach
- provide more self-expressive materials (art, pretend play, music, and movement props)
- label as many objects as possible and describe what we're doing

Family member(s):

Antoinette (Matthew's mother) will expect Matt to participate more in dressing himself. She'll try to allow more time so he and she are not so rushed in this process.

She set a goal for herself to work with Matt so he will not hit her or others. She will firmly express her displeasure and let Matt know that she expects him to tell her what's bothering him.

Our response at school will be to watch closely for this behavior and give Matt more options to express himself without hitting. If we see him hit Antoinette at drop-off or pickup time, we'll step in and support her by doing the same coaching as we would if he hit another child.

> Excerpts of a Family/Teacher Conference

(Provided by Caitlin Salpietra of University of Southern Maine Child Care Center.)

We include these excerpts to give a sense of the give-and-take nature of the conversation in a family/teacher conference centered on a portfolio. Here is Caitlin's opening conversation with the parents of Andrew (an eleven-month-old), a discussion of a specific area of development, and her closing discussion with Andrew's mother and father.

In this first section, Caitlin welcomes Andrew's parents and begins discussion of the developmental milestones around communicating:

Caitlin: *Welcome! Andrew has been a delight. It's really nice to have families with more kids—because we know you already and have that foundation. Andrew has been such fun to watch. He's changed so much. And I think this [conference] will cover it—some of the biggest changes. . . . It's been exciting.*

Mom: *One thing we've noticed a lot about Andrew is that he's very interested in music. You know, we have some musical instruments at home. And he can beat the drum at a steady pace. He's using the maraca against the drum. He's finding all of these ways to use it in ways that I would never think.*

Caitlin: *He's discovered our heater as well—you know, that grate that covers our heater? All the kids get on that. He picked up a rattle and went up and down, and up and down, tapping on it. And, those little wind-up radios that we have? He shakes those up and down and has been giving that to us because he can't turn the little thing and he wants to hear that. And he has been responding to the music that we play. He seems to like things that have a good beat going on.*

This is our portfolio that we've put together on him. And I'm going to give you each a copy of our written form to read over. You may take this home for a few weeks and go over it. We'd just like it back. . . . I'll conference with you one more time, then it will move with Andrew to the Toddler Room. I'll make a copy for you to keep. In addition, please keep these extra photos of him. You can take those copies home, but we'll keep this in here for his portfolio.

Mom: *Okay.*

Caitlin: *Communicates. Now, this is early on. . . . He'd initiate the contact with the caregiver. He'd look over and catch your eye and start smiling. This is Andrew. He likes to be talked to. He's babbling now. Yesterday, he was so funny, he was pushing that walker and talking as he was going. He's looking at books now and babbling as he's looking at things.*

Mom: *Yes.*

Caitlin: *But the language in the last few weeks has shot up. The babble is becoming longer.*

Mom: *Yeah, we were reading a book last night, a book about a bear getting dressed, and on each page he puts on a new article of clothing. So on one page he puts on his shirt and his pants. So we get to the next page and he puts on a sweater. But you could still see the shirt, and Andrew points to the shirt and said, "Shirt."*

Caitlin: *Wow, oh, wow!*

Mom: *It sounded like "shirt."*

Caitlin: *I think it was. Sometimes I think with him we're saying, "No, that couldn't be it." But I think he's saying a lot—he's got a lot of language. It's not always consistent that he's using it, but he's got it there.*

Mom: *Yeah, like with "Mama," he said that quite a while ago but he doesn't use it very often. He's kind of . . .*

Caitlin: *Collecting. . . .*

Mom: *Collecting a lot of words. This was really obvious because he was pointing to it, and it sounded exactly like "shirt."*

Caitlin: *I'm sure it was. Wow, that's exciting. Fun times.*

In the next part of the excerpt, Caitlin ends the conference and says good-bye to Andrew's parents.

Caitlin: *Here are some photos that I like.*

Dad: *Oh, he's so cute. What a cute little guy.*

Mom: *What a sweet face.*

Caitlin: *He's really right on target with everything. There are no concerns that we have on our part. Is there anything that you're . . . questions?*

Mom: *No, I think until recently I was a little concerned that he wasn't communicating verbally very much. He was pretty quiet at home. You know, part of that is that there's just so much going on, there's so much activity. He's just watching it all and taking it in. But in the last month, or month or two, he's really started to communicate with me verbally.*

Caitlin: *He has quite a bit. And, you're right, he was being very quiet, and all of a sudden . . .*

Mom: *And I started to worry: uh-oh, he's not going to be a verbal child. He's not going to express to me what he wants. He's always expressed—you could see on his face what his mood was, but he wasn't expressing verbally. And I think my concerns are over there.*

Caitlin: *Yes, I think you're right. Yes, indeed. He's quite something. He very freely expresses himself.*

Dad: *He lets you know what he wants. Neil was always a more easygoing guy. But he's a very determined little man and if you try to stop him from doing something he wants to do, he does let you know.*

Caitlin: *And that's a good thing.*

Dad: *It is a good thing.*

Caitlin: *He's been a lot of fun. He's loving; at the same time, he's independent. Likes to do things for himself. Likes to get things. But when he's ready, he likes to snuggle. . . . So basically in the coming months we'll be referring to our list of milestones that we'll be working on with him and providing him the opportunity to work on that himself.*

Mom: *I think you've done a wonderful job. He obviously loves coming to day care every day.*

Caitlin: *He's very comfortable. . . . As always, any concerns you have, please bring them to our attention. Please feel free to keep this for a while. Just return it when you're done. This will move with him when he transitions to the Toddler Room.*

Dad: *About 18 months?*

Caitlin: *Yes, about then.*

Mom: *For me, I like calling every day. And I hope that's okay.*

Caitlin: *I think it's great. And I encourage and use you as an example and tell new parents, "You know, I have a parent whose child has been in this program almost a year, and whose older child was, and continues to call. And, I said, I think it makes you happier at work to know that you can call. And, it's never a problem. The phone's right there. It stretches a long way between the kitchen and the playroom. . . . I encourage that. It makes your day go a lot better.*

Mom: *And it's convenient for me to have some time at work to just sit and think about family. It's a nice break and it helps me to hear how he's doing and it makes me feel more connected, I guess.*

Caitlin: *Great. You can call as many times as you feel like it. I like that. I like that you call and that we're there. I like being accessible, especially for parents of infants, for any age group, but infants especially. Anything else?*

Dad: *No, I don't think so.*

Caitlin: *Okay.*

chapter 10

Favorites Collection Form
Child's Name Brandon
Observer Beth
Date October 1998

> The Second Collection and Conference

You made it through your first collection. Before you begin your second collection, there are some things to think about. Because you know your children better, and because you have more familiarity with the portfolio process, there will be some changes in your thinking and focus this second time around.

The second collection of portfolio items has a purpose that the first collection did not: to document progress. Because you already have a portfolio filled with information about the child's development, you can now work toward showing how the child is growing and changing in comparison to the documentation you collected before. Knowing the children allows you to begin the second collection with individualized plans for every child in the group. In this chapter we will give you the steps to go through the second collection with this new focus and to prepare to conference with families using the Reflection and Planning Form: Final Collection.

> Documenting Favorites, Friends, and Family in the Second Collection

In the second collection, you have a choice. You can intentionally choose to document something different about the child's favorites, friends, and family, or you can choose to continue to document along similar lines, showing more depth and detail or growth on the part of the child. To begin, refer back to each child's portfolio. As you organize your collection forms for Favorites, Friends, and Family, look carefully at the items previously collected for each of the children and decide how you will use them.

> The Starting Point for Documenting Developmental Milestones

The milestones on which the child is working provide you with direction and a place to start in the second collection. They become the primary focus for your planning and observations. Refer back to the Reflection and Planning Form. On that form, you identified developmental milestones that were not yet fully accomplished or strongly developed. You identified ways that you and your colleagues would target the development of these skills and behaviors through carefully planned activities. Those experiences were designed to provide opportunities for the child to increase competence in specific areas. As you observe during the second collection, your documentation can show whether or not the child has made progress toward achieving any of those same skills. As children do achieve those milestones, you can move on and document other skills that are developing. Be alert for indications of progress in new areas too.

You will not limit yourself to only documenting the milestones on which the child is working for the entire second collection. Over the course of a few months, children develop competency in many areas simultaneously. You want portfolios to show this richness and complexity and to capture as many facets of the child's learning as you are able to document. If you limit your second collection to only those few milestones that were challenging for each child at the beginning, your portfolios will not reflect other development that occurs over the course of the whole collection. You want the portfolios to be as comprehensive as possible.

> Preparing for the Second Collection

Just as they did for the first collection, teachers must prepare for the process of collection a second time. Making copies of the collection forms for Favorites, Friends, and Family, as well as for Developmental Milestones, helps you to capture documentation quickly and efficiently. Placing the forms in each child's file can be helpful. If you find it easier to have a variety of these forms available around the classroom, make sure you have made extra photocopies and arranged for easy access.

You may want to prepare the next set of Developmental Milestones Collection Forms by writing in the milestones that the child is working on. This will keep the next steps for each child front and center for you and your colleagues. You will know exactly what you want to begin monitoring and working toward for each child. This preparation step is optional, however. If, over the course of the collection, additional milestones in the same area of development are accomplished, they can be added to the forms at a later time.

If you would rather be more open-ended as you observe the child, simply prepare collection forms that have the child's name on them. That way, as you observe and document, you can pay attention to milestones on which the child is working, as well as other milestones that the child is accomplishing.

Changes in Your Thinking

A few key factors influence your thinking as you move into your second collection. You know the children much better now than you did at the start of your first collection. You documented information about them in your anecdotes, but you also retain much of what you know about each child in your mind. You have identified children's strengths and interests. And you are aware of areas where they need support. You have begun to recognize when and how they need to be challenged to try new experiences. And you have become sensitive to their particular personalities and learning styles.

Now your job is to link your existing knowledge with the goal of documenting progress. Ask yourself: "What is this child doing differently in this area of development than he did in the first collection?"

Your reflection, along with the developmental milestone information from the first collection, helps guide your documentation of progress.

Highlighting Progress by Comparing the Past to the Present

You may refer to observations from the previous collection in the anecdotes you are writing now. Making a connection to skills and abilities demonstrated by the child in the past helps you describe any differences in what the child is doing now.

When writing an anecdote for the second collection, you can begin the anecdote with phrases such as:

"In the fall, Jeremy did . . ."

"Previously, Anna often chose to . . ."

Then you proceed to write about what the child is doing currently:

"Now, she does . . . For example, today she . . ."

You still report the facts of your observation—what you saw the child do or heard the child say. However, you are adding some historical information about what you have seen the child do in the past. This helps you and family members see progress in the child's accomplishment of developmental milestones.

On the following pages are samples (Alexandra and Abdi) that include references to past observations.

As the second collection period proceeds, you and your colleagues will be tracking progress and will be able to adjust plans accordingly for each child. Ultimately, you and the family members will be able to review the two sets of portfolio items and clearly see the changes in the child's performance.

Developmental Milestones Collection Form
Version #1 Infant/Toddler

Child's Name ALEXANDRA Age 2 YRS. 9 MOS.

Observer SARA Date APRIL 1, 1999

Check off the *areas of development* that apply:

- ❑ Shows interest in others
- ❑ Demonstrates self-awareness
- ❑ Accomplishes gross-motor milestones
- ❑ Accomplishes fine-motor milestones
- ❑ Communicates
- ❑ Acts with purpose and uses tools
- ☒ Expresses feelings

This photo, work sample and/or anecdote illustrates the following *developmental milestone(s)*:

Uses words & simple phrases to show some feelings; Expresses emotions with increasing self-control

Check off whatever applies to the context of this observation:

- ☒ Child-initiated activity
- ❑ Teacher-initiated activity
- ☒ New task for this child
- ❑ Familiar task for this child
- ❑ Done independently
- ❑ Done with adult guidance
- ☒ Done with peer(s)
- ❑ Time spent (1-5 mins.)
- ❑ Time spent (5-15 mins.)
- ❑ Time spent (15+ mins.)

Anecdotal Note: Describe what you saw the child do and/or heard the child say.

IN THE FALL, ALEX WAS NON-VERBAL IN HER COMMUNICATION WITH OTHER CHILDREN, SHOWING HER FEELINGS MOSTLY THROUGH BEHAVIOR RATHER THAN WORDS. TODAY, SHE USED MANY WORDS. SHE WAS PLAYING IN THE PRETEND AREA WHEN ZAHAVA TOOK AWAY THE CRADLE SHE WAS PLAYING WITH. SHE TURNED TO ZAHAVA AND SAID, "I DON'T LIKE IT WHEN YOU TAKE MY TOY!"

ZAHAVA DID NOT GIVE THE CRADLE BACK. ALEX CAME TO ME AND SAID, "SARA, SHE HAS MY CRADLE. I HAD IT FIRST!" TOGETHER, WE WENT OVER TO ZAHAVA. I URGED ALEX TO REPEAT HER FORMER MESSAGE. I NODDED AND STAYED CLOSE WHILE THIS WAS GOING ON. EVENTUALLY, THE CRADLE WAS RETURNED. TWO MINUTES LATER, ALEX SAID TO ZAHAVA: "HERE, YOU CAN PLAY WITH IT. I FINISHED."

Developmental Milestones Collection Form
Version #1 Preschooler

Child's Name Abdi Age five years
Observer Marion Date Feb. 26, 1999

Check off the *areas of development* that apply:

- ❑ Thinking, Reasoning & Problem-Solving
- ❑ Emotional and Social Competency
- ❑ Gross-Motor Development
- ❑ Fine-Motor Development
- ❑ Language and Communication
- ☑ Reading & Writing Development
- ❑ Creative Development

This photo, work sample and/or anecdote illustrates the following *developmental milestone(s):*

Role plays self as reader, relying heavily on memory, pictures and/or some word recognition.

Check off whatever applies to the context of this observation:

- ☑ Child-initiated activity
- ❑ Teacher-initiated activity
- ❑ New task for this child
- ☑ Familiar task for this child
- ☑ Done independently
- ❑ Done with adult guidance
- ❑ Done with peer(s)
- ❑ Time spent (1-5 mins.)
- ☑ Time spent (5-15 mins.)
- ❑ Time spent (15+ mins.)

Anecdotal Note: Describe what you saw the child do and/or heard the child say.

By December, Abdi was frequently found in the reading corner with books, which he read from memory, relying on the pictures as clues. Today, he took the book, Where the Wild Things Are, from the shelf and headed to the reading corner. Once there, he settled himself on a rug, turned to the title page, pointed to the title and the author's name and said them out loud. He turned to the first page of the story and while pointing to the print, recited the text accurately. His finger moved across the print and was not synchronized with the words he was saying.

> Conferencing with Families after the Second Collection Is Complete

Family/teacher conferences will have a different focus the second time around. Hopefully, there will be progress to report in several areas. In some cases, there may be comments and documentation about the child's need for special support and help. Or you may identify that more time is needed for the child to solidify a skill. These teacher comments all reflect a typical range of development that will be evident in each portfolio.

The major difference between the first and second conferences will be the ability of both parties to compare the child's earlier performance to what she currently does. All parties will be in a position to make the connection between the planning strategies and goals written on the Reflection and Planning Form and any changes in the child's performance. Family members and teachers will be able to exchange stories of support and interventions that were used with the child at home and at school. The second conference will focus on analyzing the progress seen, beginning with reference to the milestones on which the child was working, and then including stories about the child's overall growth, interests, and learning.

We recommend that this conference be used to summarize the child's progress and accomplishments over the last nine or ten months. For this purpose, we have designed a different reporting form called the Focused Portfolios™ Reflection and Planning Form: Final Collection. This form follows on the next pages.

Focused Portfolios™ Reflection and Planning Form Final Collection

Child's Name ____________________ Age ____ Teacher ____________________ Date _________

Teacher Reflection

Refer to all *areas of development* and to the items in the portfolio

Summarize information from Favorites, Friends, and Family:

List milestones accomplished:

Describe progress observed as compared to previous collection(s):

Milestones that this child is working on:

General Comments about This Child's Growth and Development Over the Course of the Year

Teacher:

Family member(s):

Using the Final Collection Form

You can see that the first page of this form is very similar to the reflection page used previously. Once again, teachers identify favorites and list milestones accomplished by the child. They also describe progress observed.

However, this time, there is an added phrase to consider—"compared to previous collection(s)." In noting any progress, teachers first pay attention to the milestones they identified in earlier collections. Then they consider overall developmental gains made by the child. In this section on the form, they answer questions such as

- "Did the child make progress on any of those milestones that were difficult or just emerging for him?"
- "How did he show that progress?"
- "What progress was evident in other milestones or areas of development?"
- "What was observed that led to this conclusion about the child's growth?"

You needn't limit yourself to writing about the milestones that were more challenging for the child in the last collection; however, you want to be sure to address them first. Once that's done, note any other areas of significant progress you have observed.

The last section of the Reflection page is the same as was used for previous collections. Children are always learning new things and developing new skills. Noting milestones that are emerging, or coming along for each child, will provide family members and future teachers with the most current information about the child's ongoing development.

The final family/teacher conference is a time to summarize the child's overall growth and development; therefore, the second page of the form for the Final Collection is not focused on planning as the other was. There is space for both teachers and family members to write general comments and thoughts about the child's total experience in the classroom. These general comments can address a wide array of topics. Some that might be considered by you and each child's family members can include the following:

- Summarizing what you have learned about this child as a person: unique characteristics, approaches to learning, likes and dislikes, strengths, interests, and personality traits.
- Addressing the work done both at home and school as a result of the plans made together in earlier conferences. This is a way to celebrate the partnership you and the family have built on behalf of the child.

- Reflecting on the child's emerging competencies, as shown in the portfolio.
- Sharing an additional story or anecdote about the child.
- Making personal comments about your relationship with the child and her family.
- Sharing your perception of the child's experience in your classroom.

On the following pages you will find Cara's Reflection and Planning Form: Final Collection. You may want to refer back to chapter 9 to review the form for the first collection of Cara's portfolio. Then you can compare the similarities and differences, see the changes that were documented, and read how this progress was reported.

Focused Portfolios™ Reflection and Planning Form
Final Collection

Child's Name Cara Age 5½ Teacher Maria Date 5/99

Teacher Reflection

Refer to all *areas of development* and to the items in the portfolio

Summarize information from Favorites, Friends, and Family:

Cara and Taylor frequently announce that they are best friends, and this is very evident to us. They play at reading and writing and dance, and continue to enjoy pretend play. They always sit together at snack. Grandpa's visit made a lasting impression—Cara is still talking about it!

List milestones accomplished:

- sustains interest in a task, and works hard to solve problems independently or with some adult coaching and support
- demonstrates interest in exploring aspects of home, school, and community
- sorts objects by two or more attributes
- remembers and recites poems, songs, and stories and acts them out
- reads print in the environment (many classmates' names, alphabet letters in the newspaper, classroom labels)
- is curious about letters and words
- responds to music through rhythmic, controlled body movements
- explores a variety of expressive media with purpose, often with a product in mind
- sometimes names a thing in a drawing

Describe progress observed as compared to previous collection(s):

- plays with "best friend" (Taylor) extensively
- uses complex sentence structure and has the vocabulary to express most wants, needs, and explanations without difficulty
- role plays self as reader, relying heavily on memory, pictures, and some word recognition
- uses writing tools with more control

Milestones that this child is working on:

- draws persons and geometric designs (Cara's general fine-motor control with writing and drawing tools is improving. She would benefit from lots more practice and experiences with pencils, pens, markers, and crayons)
- groups items into higher order categories and classes of objects
- prints first name (often writes CRAA) and prints some letters crudely but readably for adults

General Comments about This Child's Growth and Development Over the Course of the Year

Teacher:

Cara started the year with so many skills and competencies. Her language development and social skills have continued to grow. Her awareness and interest in reading and writing have increased. Art is a special activity for Cara—she chooses it often. Her general physical coordination is strong.

Cara can still be challenged to count to higher quantities, sort objects into more categories than just size and color, and to continue to solve problems independently. She loves to learn and will benefit from any activities, games, and reading times her family members do with her.

Family member(s):

Cara has really enjoyed preschool this year. She has learned so much and always wants to come to school. We think she'll really miss it.

We did make a Writing Box for her at home and she writes all the time. We've noticed that the way she writes her name is getting better.

Thank you, Maria, for all you've done for Cara and the other children.

Cara's Mom and Dad

> Using the Final Reflection Form after the Summer Collection in a Year-Round Program

If children attend your program in the summer months, you may decide to complete the Final Reflection Form to accompany whatever portfolio items were collected during that time. Because summer curriculum and schedules are more relaxed, we recognize that this collection may not be as extensive as earlier ones.

If completing the Final Reflection Form at the end of the summer, teachers can choose to summarize only what the child did in June, July, and August. Or, if they know the child well and are familiar with previous collections, their summary can refer to those as well. Again, we trust that administration and staff will decide accordingly which forms are appropriate to use at the end of the summer session.

> Giving the Portfolio to the Family

As at other family/teacher conferences, family members receive a copy of the completed Reflection and Planning Form: Final Collection, and a copy remains at the program as a permanent record of the child's development. In a nine- or ten-month program, the portfolio (or a copy) may go home with the family after the second or final conference. In a twelve-month program, a decision must be made about when to send the portfolios home.

Some year-round programs choose to keep the portfolios at the center as long as the child attends. This way, a continuous record is built describing the child's development. When the child leaves the program, the portfolio goes home with the family.

Another option is to have each of the child's new teachers review the previous year's portfolio before sending it home with the family. Others in year-round programs send the portfolios home after either the second conference or the summer one. Then, whether or not the child has a new teacher, a new collection is started in the fall.

> Family Reactions

The documentation you have carefully organized now becomes a significant part of the family's history of the child's growth and development. Teachers report that families take great pride and ownership in the photographs, anecdotes, and work samples. They see their child's progress in pictures and stories right before their eyes. Family members also report how enlightening and helpful the portfolios are in seeing their children's progress in all areas. Families of children with identified special needs find that portfolio items that are tied to Individual Family Service Plan or Individual Education Plan goals provide a clear picture of what their children can do. They say they feel more hopeful because the documentation in the portfolio focuses on success rather than failure (even if those successes are below chronological age expectations).

This final conference is a celebration of the child. Presenting the completed portfolio as a gift to the family cements the connection between you and the family, and demonstrates the valuable work you do on behalf of children.

appendixes

Favorites Collection Form
Child's Name Brandon
Observer Beth
Date October 1998

> Appendix A:
Focused Portfolios™ Forms

Forms on the following pages may be reproduced
for use in portfolios.

Friends Collection Form

Child's Name ______________________ Date ______________________

Observer ______________________

Based on your observations, who are this child's friends? What do they do together? How does this child express his or her feelings towards them? Add a photo to illustrate this friendship.

Description:

Favorites Collection Form

Child's Name ______________________________ Date ________________________

Observer ________________________

After observing the child on multiple occasions, describe a favorite activity that the child does often. Add details that you've noticed about the child's interests and choices. Add a photo if you can.

Description:

Family Collection Form

Child's Name ______________________________ Date ________________________

Observer ________________________

Families often have stories to share about their child's accomplishments at home. They also have special moments with their child in your classroom. Use this form to document a story that the child's family has shared with you, or take a photo of a special moment between the child and the people who are important in his or her life.

Description:

Focused Portfolios™ Photo

Attach
photograph
here

Developmental Milestones Collection Form
Version #1 Infant/Toddler

Child's Name ______________________________ Age ______________

Observer ______________________________ Date ______________

Check off the *areas of development* that apply:

- ❑ Shows interest in others
- ❑ Demonstrates self-awareness
- ❑ Accomplishes gross-motor milestones
- ❑ Accomplishes fine-motor milestones
- ❑ Communicates
- ❑ Acts with purpose and uses tools
- ❑ Expresses feelings

This photo, work sample and/or anecdote illustrates the following *developmental milestone(s):*

____

____

____

____

Check off whatever applies to the context of this observation:

- ❑ Child-initiated activity
- ❑ Teacher-initiated activity
- ❑ New task for this child
- ❑ Familiar task for this child
- ❑ Done independently
- ❑ Done with adult guidance
- ❑ Done with peer(s)
- ❑ Time spent (1–5 mins.)
- ❑ Time spent (5–15 mins.)
- ❑ Time spent (15+ mins.)

Anecdotal Note: Describe what you saw the child do and/or heard the child say.

Developmental Milestones Collection Form
Version #1 Preschooler

Child's Name ______________________________ Age ____________

Observer ______________________________ Date ____________

Check off the *areas of development* that apply:

- ❑ Thinking, Reasoning & Problem-Solving
- ❑ Emotional and Social Competency
- ❑ Gross-Motor Development
- ❑ Fine-Motor Development
- ❑ Language and Communication
- ❑ Reading & Writing Development
- ❑ Creative Development

This photo, work sample and/or anecdote illustrates the following *developmental milestone(s):*

____

____

____

____

Check off whatever applies to the context of this observation:

❑ Child-initiated activity	❑ Done with adult guidance
❑ Teacher-initiated activity	❑ Done with peer(s)
❑ New task for this child	❑ Time spent (1–5 mins.)
❑ Familiar task for this child	❑ Time spent (5–15 mins.)
❑ Done independently	❑ Time spent (15+ mins.)

Anecdotal Note: Describe what you saw the child do and/or heard the child say.

Developmental Milestones Collection Form
Version #2 Infant/Toddler
(using your own developmental charts)

Child's Name ________________________ Age ________

Observer ________________________ Date ________

List the *areas of development* that apply:

____

____

____

This photo, work sample and/or anecdote illustrates the following *developmental milestone(s):*

____

____

____

Check off whatever applies to the context of this observation:

- ❑ Child-initiated activity
- ❑ Teacher-initiated activity
- ❑ New task for this child
- ❑ Familiar task for this child
- ❑ Done independently
- ❑ Done with adult guidance
- ❑ Done with peer(s)
- ❑ Time spent (1–5 mins.)
- ❑ Time spent (5–15 mins.)
- ❑ Time spent (15+ mins.)

Anecdotal Note: Describe what you saw the child do and/or heard the child say.

Developmental Milestones Collection Form
Version #2 Preschooler
(using your own developmental charts)

Child's Name ______________________________ Age ____________

Observer ______________________________ Date ____________

List the *areas of development* that apply:

____

____

____

This photo, work sample and/or anecdote illustrates the following *developmental milestone(s):*

____

____

____

Check off whatever applies to the context of this observation:

- ❑ Child-initiated activity
- ❑ Teacher-initiated activity
- ❑ New task for this child
- ❑ Familiar task for this child
- ❑ Done independently
- ❑ Done with adult guidance
- ❑ Done with peer(s)
- ❑ Time spent (1–5 mins.)
- ❑ Time spent (5–15 mins.)
- ❑ Time spent (15+ mins.)

Anecdotal Note: Describe what you saw the child do and/or heard the child say.

Developmental Milestones Collection Form
Version #3 Infant/Toddler
(for young children with identified special needs)

Child's Name ______________________________ Age ____________

Observer ______________________________ Date ____________

List the *areas of development* that apply:

____

____

____

This photo, work sample and/or anecdote illustrates the following IFSP goals:

____

____

____

Check off whatever applies to the context of this observation:

- ❑ Child-initiated activity
- ❑ Teacher-initiated activity
- ❑ New task for this child
- ❑ Familiar task for this child
- ❑ Done independently
- ❑ Done with adult guidance
- ❑ Done with peer(s)
- ❑ Time spent (1–5 mins.)
- ❑ Time spent (5–15 mins.)
- ❑ Time spent (15+ mins.)

Anecdotal Note: Describe what you saw the child do and/or heard the child say.

Developmental Milestones Collection Form
Version #3 Preschooler
(for young children with identified special needs)

Child's Name ______________________________ Age ____________

Observer ______________________________ Date ____________

List the *areas of development* that apply:

____

____

____

This photo, work sample and/or anecdote illustrates the following IEP goals:

____

____

____

Check off whatever applies to the context of this observation:

- ❑ Child-initiated activity
- ❑ Teacher-initiated activity
- ❑ New task for this child
- ❑ Familiar task for this child
- ❑ Done independently
- ❑ Done with adult guidance
- ❑ Done with peer(s)
- ❑ Time spent (1–5 mins.)
- ❑ Time spent (5–15 mins.)
- ❑ Time spent (15+ mins.)

Anecdotal Note: Describe what you saw the child do and/or heard the child say.

Infant/Toddler Word List

Child ______________________ Teacher(s) ______________________

Date:	Word Approximations, Words, and/or Word Combinations	Context (imitation, response to comment or question, self-initiated)

Anecdotal Comments:

Focused Portfolios™ Reflection and Planning Form

Child's Name ____________________ Age _______ Teacher ________________ Date ________

Teacher Reflection

Refer to all *areas of development* and to the items in the portfolio

Summarize information from Favorites, Friends, and Family:

List milestones accomplished:

Describe progress that has been observed:

List the milestones that this child is working on (these are the goals for the next collection):

Family and Teacher Planning

Discuss plans to support further development. Write ideas for classroom activities, family involvement, and teacher support. Add any general comments.

Teacher:

Family member(s):

Focused Portfolios™ Reflection and Planning Form
Final Collection

Child's Name ____________________ Age ____ Teacher ____________________ Date _________

Teacher Reflection

Refer to all *areas of development* and to the items in the portfolio

Summarize information from Favorites, Friends, and Family:

List milestones accomplished:

Describe progress observed as compared to previous collection(s):

Milestones that this child is working on:

General Comments about This Child's Growth and Development Over the Course of the Year

Teacher:

Family member(s):

Focused Portfolios™

Recording Class Observations by Date
Infant/Toddler

Instructions for using this form: Enter the names of all children in the group. Working across the page, write the dates of your observations in the appropriate columns.

Child's Name	Shows Interest in Others	Demonstrates Self-Awareness	Gross-Motor Development	Fine-Motor Development	Communicates	Acts with Purpose and Uses Tools	Expresses Feelings

Focused Portfolios™

Recording Class Observations by Date
Preschooler

Instructions for using this form: Enter the names of all children in the group. Working across the page, write the dates of your observations in the appropriate columns.

Child's Name	Thinking, Reasoning, and Problem Solving	Emotional and Social Competency	Language and Communication	Gross-Motor Development	Fine-Motor Development	Reading and Writing Development	Creative Development

Focused Portfolios™

Recording Individual Child Observations by Date
Infant/Toddler

Child's Name ________________________________

Instructions for using this form: Place this form on the outside of each child's portfolio folder. As you record and file observation documentation in the child's folder, write the dates of your observations in the appropriate columns.

Documentation Collected	Date(s) for Fall Collection	Date(s) for Spring Collection
Favorites		
Friends		
Family		
Shows Interest in Others		
Demonstrates Self-Awareness		
Gross-Motor Development		
Fine-Motor Development		
Communicates		
Acts with Purpose and Uses Tools		
Expresses Feelings		

Focused Portfolios™

Recording Individual Child Observations by Date
Preschoolers

Child's Name ______________________________

Instructions for using this form: Place this form on the outside of each child's portfolio folder. As you record and file observation documentation in the child's folder, write the dates of your observations in the appropriate columns.

Documentation Collected	Date(s) for Fall Collection	Date(s) for Spring Collection
Favorites		
Friends		
Family		
Thinking, Reasoning, and Problem-Solving		
Emotional and Social Competency		
Language and Communication		
Gross-Motor Development		
Fine-Motor Development		
Reading and Writing Development		
Creative Development		

Tracking Progress through Multiple Anecdotes

Child's Name ______________________ Area of Development ______________________

Anecdotal Note: Describe what you saw the child do and/or heard the child say.

Date:____________Child's age______________Observer______________________

Anecdotal Note: Describe what you saw the child do and/or heard the child say.

Date:____________Child's age______________Observer______________________

Anecdotal Note: Describe what you saw the child do and/or heard the child say.

Date:____________Child's age______________Observer______________________

> Appendix B:

Focused Portfolios™ Forms in Spanish

Forms on the following pages may be reproduced for use in portfolios.

Formulario de colección de amigos

Nombre del Niño(a) ______________________________ Fecha ____________________________

Observador______________________________

Basado en sus observaciones, ¿quiénes son los amigos de este niño(a)? ¿Qué hacen juntos? ¿Cómo expresa este niño(a) sus sentimientos hacia ellos? Agregue una foto para ilustrar esta amistad.

Descripción:

Formulario de colección de favoritos

Nombre del Niño(a) ______________________________ Fecha ____________________________

Observador____________________________

Luego de observar al niño(a) en múltiples ocasiones, describa una actividad favorita que el niño(a) hace con frecuencia. Agregue detalles que usted ha notado acerca de los intereses y gustos del niño(a). Agregue una foto si es posible.

Descripción:

Formulario de colección de familia

Nombre del Niño(a) ______________________________ Fecha ____________________________

Observador____________________________

Las familias por lo regular tienen historias que compartir acerca de los logros de sus hijos en casa. También tienen momentos especiales con sus hijos en el salón de clase. Use este formulario para documentar una historia que hayan compartido con usted, o para tomar una foto y describir un momento especial entre el niño(a) y aquellos que son muy importantes en su vida.

Descripción:

Foto de Focused Portfolios™

Pegue la
fotografía aquí

Formulario de colección de etapas del desarrollo
Versión #1 Bebés/ Nenes

Nombre del Niño(a) ______________________ Edad __________

Observador ______________________ Fecha __________

Marque las áreas de desarrollo apropiadas:

- ❑ Demuestra interés en los demás
- ❑ Demuestra auto-conciencia
- ❑ Logra habilidades motoras generales
- ❑ Logra habilidades motoras finas
- ❑ Se comunica
- ❑ Actúa con propósito y usa herramientas
- ❑ Expresa sus sentimientos

Esta foto y/o anécdota ilustra las siguientes etapas del desarrollo:

____

____

____

____

Marque cualquier cosa que se relacione con el contexto de esta observación:

- ❑ El niño inició la actividad
- ❑ La maestra inició la actividad
- ❑ Nueva actividad para este niño
- ❑ Actividad conocida para este niño
- ❑ Lo hizo independientemente
- ❑ Lo hizo con ayuda de un adulto
- ❑ Lo hizo con otro(s) niño(s)
- ❑ Tiempo consumido (1–5 m.)
- ❑ Tiempo consumido (5–15 m.)
- ❑ Tiempo consumido (15 o más m.)

Nota anecdótica: Describa lo que vió al niño hacer y/u oyó al niño decir.

Formulario de colección de etapas del desarrollo
Versión #1 Preescolar

Nombre del Niño(a) ______________________ Edad __________

Observador ______________________ Fecha __________

Marque las áreas de desarrollo apropiadas:

- ❑ Pensar, razonar y resolver problemas
- ❑ Es competente emocional y socialmente
- ❑ Desarrollo motor general
- ❑ Desarrollo motor fino
- ❑ Lenguaje y comunicación
- ❑ Desarrollo de lectura y escritura
- ❑ Desarrollo creativo

Esta foto y/o anécdota ilustra las siguientes etapas del desarrollo:

____

____

____

____

Marque cualquier cosa que se relacione con el contexto de esta observación:

- ❑ El niño inició la actividad
- ❑ La maestra inició la actividad
- ❑ Nueva actividad para este niño
- ❑ Actividad conocida para este niño
- ❑ Lo hizo independientemente
- ❑ Lo hizo con ayuda de un adulto
- ❑ Lo hizo con otro(s) niño(s)
- ❑ Tiempo consumido (1–5 m.)
- ❑ Tiempo consumido (5–15 m.)
- ❑ Tiempo consumido (15 o más m.)

Nota anecdótica: Describa lo que vió al niño hacer y/u oyó al niño decir.

Formulario de colección de etapas del desarrollo
Versión #2 Bebés/ Nenes
(Usando sus propias tablas del desarrollo)

Nombre del Niño(a) ______________________ Edad __________

Observador ______________________ Fecha __________

Anote las áreas de desarrollo apropiadas:

____

____

____

Esta foto y/o anécdota ilustra las siguientes etapas del desarrollo:

____

____

____

Marque cualquier cosa que se relacione con el contexto de esta observación:

- ❑ El niño inició la actividad
- ❑ La maestra inició la actividad
- ❑ Nueva actividad para este niño
- ❑ Actividad conocida para este niño
- ❑ Lo hizo independientemente
- ❑ Lo hizo con ayuda de un adulto
- ❑ Lo hizo con otro(s) niño(s)
- ❑ Tiempo consumido (1–5 m.)
- ❑ Tiempo consumido (5–15 m.)
- ❑ Tiempo consumido (15 o más m.)

Nota anecdótica: Describa lo que vió al niño hacer y/u oyó al niño decir.

Formulario de colección de etapas del desarrollo
Versión #2 Preescolar
(Usando sus propias tablas del desarrollo)

Nombre del Niño(a) ______________________________ Edad ______________

Observador ______________________________ Fecha ______________

Anote las áreas de desarrollo apropiadas:

____

____

____

Esta foto y/o anécdota ilustra las siguientes etapas del desarrollo:

____

____

____

Marque cualquier cosa que se relacione con el contexto de esta observación:

- ❑ El niño inició la actividad
- ❑ La maestra inició la actividad
- ❑ Nueva actividad para este niño
- ❑ Actividad conocida para este niño
- ❑ Lo hizo independientemente
- ❑ Lo hizo con ayuda de un adulto
- ❑ Lo hizo con otro(s) niño(s)
- ❑ Tiempo consumido (1–5 m.)
- ❑ Tiempo consumido (5–15 m.)
- ❑ Tiempo consumido (15 o más m.)

Nota anecdótica: Describa lo que vió al niño hacer y/u oyó al niño decir.

Formulario de comentarios y planificación del Focused Portfolios™

Nombre del Niño____________________ Edad________ Maestra__________________ Fecha___________

Comentarios de la Maestra

Haga referencia a todas las áreas del desarrollo y los objetos en el portafolio

Resuma la información de los formularios de Favoritos, Amigos y Familia:

Anote las etapas cumplidas:

Describa el progreso que ha observado:

Anote las etapas en las que este niño está mejorando (estas son las metas para la siguiente colección):

Planificación de la familia y de la maestra

Platiquen sobre los planes para fomentar un mejor desarrollo. Escriban ideas para actividades en el salón, participación familiar y apoyo de la maestra. Agregue cualquier comentario general.

Maestra:

Miembro(s) de la familia:

Formulario de comentarios y Planificación del Focused Portfolios™ Colección Final

Nombre del Niño_______________________ Edad________ Maestra____________________ Fecha___________

Comentarios de la Maestra

Haga referencia a todas las áreas del desarrollo y los objetos en el portafolio

Resuma la información de los formularios de Favoritos, Amigos y Familia:

Anote las etapas cumplidas:

Describa el progreso que ha observado comparado con colecciones previas:

Anote las etapas eventos en las que este niño está mejorando:

Comentarios generales sobre el crecimiento y desarrollo de este niño(a) durante el curso del año

Maestra:

Familiares:

> Appendix C: Sample Forms Using Criteria from Other Assessment Systems

Developmental Milestones Collection Form
Version #2 Preschooler
(using your own developmental charts)

Child's Name Robbie Age 4
Observer Linda Date Sept. 30/98

List the *areas of development* that apply:

Language & Literacy
Speaking & Writing

This photo, work sample and/or anecdote illustrates the following *developmental milestone(s):*

Uses language for a variety of purposes; Uses letter-like shapes to write words

Check off whatever applies to the context of this observation:

- ☐ Child-initiated activity
- ☒ Teacher-initiated activity
- ☐ New task for this child
- ☐ Familiar task for this child
- ☐ Done independently
- ☒ Done with adult guidance
- ☐ Done with peer(s)
- ☐ Time spent (1-5 mins.)
- ☒ Time spent (5-15 mins.)
- ☐ Time spent (15+ mins.)

Anecdotal Note: Describe what you saw the child do and/or heard the child say.

Robbie drew a skeleton and showed it to me. I asked if he wanted me to write down his words about it. "Yes!" he replied. He spoke clearly and watched as I wrote. Then he asked, "Can I write too?" I asked what he wanted to write. "I want to write 'skeleton'," he said. I wrote the word on a card for him and he spent a long time copying it onto his paper.

(see attached drawing and writing)

Using the Work Sampling System®, Margo L. Dichtelmiller, et al.

Skelton
Some skeldon's are alive and some are dead.
Some people have skeldon's and Some people don't.
Robbie

Developmental Milestones Collection Form
Version #2 Preschooler
(using your own developmental charts)

Child's Name Jasmine Age 3 years old
Observer Kelly Date 10/20/98

List the *areas of development* that apply:

Using Creative Curriculum®
Social-Emotional: Cooperative, Pro-Social Behavior

This photo, work sample and/or anecdote illustrates the following *developmental milestone(s):*

works cooperatively with others in completing a task.

Check off whatever applies to the context of this observation:

- ☐ Child-initiated activity
- ☑ Teacher-initiated activity
- ☑ New task for this child
- ☐ Familiar task for this child
- ☐ Done independently
- ☐ Done with adult guidance
- ☑ Done with peer(s)
- ☐ Time spent (1-5 mins.)
- ☑ Time spent (5-15 mins.)
- ☐ Time spent (15+ mins.)

Anecdotal Note: Describe what you saw the child do and/or heard the child say.

Jasmine, Kathleen and Alese play cooperatively in many areas of the classroom, but rarely in the Block Area. Today, I suggested that the blocks be for girls only, and steered the boys to many other selections in the classroom. Jasmine and her friends cheered loudly, clapped their hands, and spent much time working together to build this structure.

Jasmine is on the lower right

> Appendix D: Quantifying and Aggregating Data from the Focused Portfolios™ Process

Many early childhood programs are required to report information about the growth and development of the children whom they serve in a quantifiable and aggregated manner. This can be done using the Focused Portfolios™ process. We are working with several programs to help them remain true to the child-focused, family-friendly emphasis of an authentic assessment tool while, at the same time, being accountable to funding or government agencies.

We have designed two methods to quantify, aggregate, and analyze data from the portfolios: rating development that is on track; and using rubrics to identify a model set of portfolio items, which can then provide detailed analytical information for each program.

Neither way asks the teacher to do anything out of the ordinary with the collection process. She still carefully observes the children in every day classroom activities. She still records factual and descriptive anecdotes and relates those anecdotes to developmental milestone information. The quantification is done at an administrative level. In the quantification process, the developmental information becomes increasingly important.

> Rating On-Track Development

The Developmental Milestones Charts included in this book are categorized by age, as are many other developmental sources that a program might choose to use as a source of age-appropriate expectations. One way to quantify the portfolio items is to relate the developmental milestone that is recorded by the teacher on the collection form to the age of the child. If the milestone selected matches the child's age, a mark of "On Track with Age-Level Expectations" is noted. If the milestone does not match the child's age, a mark of either "Above Age-Level Expectations" or "Below Age-Level Expectations" is made. This marking is not made on the collection form itself, but rather on a table used for administrative purposes only (see example below where * means "On track," + means "above," and – means "below").

Child's Name	Thinking, Reasoning & Problem Solving	Social & Emotional Competence	Gross-Motor Development	Fine-Motor Development	Language & Communication	Reading & Writing Development	Creative Development
Amber	+	–	*	*	*	–	+
Benjamin	–	*	*	+	–	*	*
Cranford	*	*	*	*	–	*	*
Danielle	*	+	–	*	*	+	*

The marks for all children in one age group are then tallied in the three categories, "on track," "above," and "below." They can be averaged by the total number of samples in that area of development for the children in that age group. After that, a percentage of children in the group who are on track, "above" and "below" can be determined.

Reporting can include information like the following: "In the fall, 40% of the four-year-olds in our program were on track with age-level expectations in the area of Fine-Motor Development; 15% were above age-level expectations; 45% were below age-level expectations." A spring report then might say, "In the spring, 60% of the four-year-olds in our program were on track with age level expectations in the area of Fine-Motor Development; 20% were above age-level expectations; 20% were below age-level expectations."

Tracking this data across two collections (fall and spring) can give the administrator of a program, and those reviewing this data for funding or regulatory purposes, information about progress that children made across the program year.

Using the On-Track Approach with Head Start Performance Standards

Head Start programs may choose to relate children's portfolios directly to the Head Start Performance Standards. These standards are considered appropriate expectations for four-year-olds. Thus, the rating and recording of a mark might be: "* Meets the Head Start Performance Standard," "+ Goes beyond the Head Start Performance Standard," "– Does not meet the Head Start Performance Standard."

> Identifying a Model Set of Portfolio Items

Identifying a model set of portfolio items is a more complex task which requires time: time to collect at least two portfolio items in several designated areas of development (with specific milestones identified), and time to analyze those items to determine specific qualities that demonstrate a child's performance of widely held expectations for specific ages.

We are in the process of working with programs on writing rubrics that define specific qualities for this analysis. We would be happy to work with other programs that would like to pursue this approach to quantification and aggregation.

If you are interested in more information, please contact us. We will work closely with administrators and teachers to help you continue your commitment to authentic assessment using the Focused Portfolios™ process. We will also help you to quantify and aggregate the data you need for funding and reporting purposes.

Contact:

Gaye Gronlund
ECE Consulting, Inc.
12005 Watermark Court
Indianapolis, IN 46236
(317) 823-8860
Email: GLGronlund@AOL.com

Bev Engel
Consultant
215 High Street #102
S. Portland, ME 04106
(207) 767-0701
E-Mail: engelschrodt@earthlink.net

Further information can be found at www.focusedportfolios.com.

> Appendix E: References

> Other Recommended Milestone Charts and Checklists

Bricker, Diane. *Assessment, Evaluation, and Programming System (AEPS) for Infants and Children.* Baltimore: Paul H. Brookes Publishing Co., 1997.

Dichtelmiller, Margo L., Judy R. Jablon, Aviva B. Dorfman, Dorothea B. Marsden, and Samuel J. Meisels. *The Work Sampling System.* Ann Arbor, Mich.: Rebus Inc., 1994.

Dodge, Diane Trister, and Laura J. Colker. *The Creative Curriculum for Early Childhood,* 3rd ed. Washington, D.C.: Teaching Strategies, Inc., 1995.

Dodge, Diane Trister, Laura J. Colker, and Cate Heroman. *The Creative Curriculum Developmental Continuum Assessment Toolkit for Ages 3–5.* Washington, D.C.: Teaching Strategies, Inc., forthcoming 2001.

Dombro, Amy Laura, Laura J. Colker, and Diane Trister Dodge. *The Creative Curriculum for Infants and Toddlers.* Washington, D.C.: Teaching Strategies, Inc., 1997.

High/Scope Educational Research Foundation. *High/Scope Child Observation Record for Ages 2–6.* Ypsilanti, Mich.: High/Scope Press, 1992.

> Reference List

Berk, Laura E., and Adam Winsler. *Scaffolding Children's Learning: Vygotsky and Early Childhood Education.* Washington, D.C.: NAEYC, 1995.

Bredekamp, Sue, and Carol Copple, eds. *Developmentally Appropriate Practice in Early Childhood Programs.* Rev. ed. Washington, D.C.: NAEYC, 1997.

Nebraska Department of Education, Iowa Department of Education, Iowa Area Education Agencies, and Head Start–State Collaboration Project. *The Primary Program: Growing and Learning in the Heartland.* Lincoln, Neb.: Nebraska Department of Education, 1993.

> Index

d

f

g

h

i

j

m

n

o

p

q

r

s